A Book Of

CORPORATE FINANCE

For
MBA Semester - IV
As Per Savitribai Phule Pune University's Revised Syllabus
Effective from June 2014

Meera Govindaraj
M.Com., MBA (Finance)

MBA : CORPORATE FINANCE　　　　　　　　　　　　　　　　**ISBN 978-93-5164-261-9**

First Edition : **December 2014**

© : **Authors**

The text of this publication, or any part thereof, should not be reproduced or transmitted in any form or stored in any computer storage system or device for distribution including photocopy, recording, taping or information retrieval system or reproduced on any disc, tape, perforated media or other information storage device etc., without the written permission of Authors with whom the rights are reserved. Breach of this condition is liable for legal action.

Every effort has been made to avoid errors or omissions in this publication. In spite of this, errors may have crept in. Any mistake, error or discrepancy so noted and shall be brought to our notice shall be taken care of in the next edition. It is notified that neither the publisher nor the authors or seller shall be responsible for any damage or loss of action to any one, of any kind, in any manner, therefrom.

Published By :
NIRALI PRAKASHAN
Abhyudaya Pragati, 1312, Shivaji Nagar,
Off J.M. Road, PUNE – 411005
Tel - (020) 25512336/37/39, Fax - (020) 25511379
Email : niralipune@pragationline.com

Printed By :
Repro Knowledgecast Limited,
Thane

DISTRIBUTION CENTRES
PUNE

Nirali Prakashan
119, Budhwar Peth, Jogeshwari Mandir Lane
Pune 411002, Maharashtra
Tel : (020) 2445 2044, 66022708, Fax : (020) 2445 1538
Email : niralilocal@pragationline.com

Nirali Prakashan
S. No. 28/27, Dhyari,
Near Pari Company, Pune 411041
Tel : (020) 24690204, Fax : (020) 24690316
Email : bookorder@pragationline.com

MUMBAI
Nirali Prakashan
385, S.V.P. Road, Rasdhara Co-op. Hsg. Society Ltd.,
Girgaum, Mumbai 400004, Maharashtra
Tel : (022) 2385 6339 / 2386 9976, Fax : (022) 2386 9976
Email : niralimumbai@pragationline.com

DISTRIBUTION BRANCHES

NAGPUR
Pratibha Book Distributors
Above Maratha Mandir, Shop No. 3, First Floor,
Rani Jhanshi Square, Sitabuldi, Nagpur 440012,
Maharashtra, Tel : (0712) 254 7129

JALGAON
Nirali Prakashan
34, V. V. Golani Market, Navi Peth, Jalgaon 425001,
Maharashtra, Tel : (0257) 222 0395
Mob : 94234 91860

BENGALURU
Pragati Book House
House No. 1, Sanjeevappa Lane, Avenue Road Cross,
Opp. Rice Church, Bengaluru – 560002.
Tel : (080) 64513344, 64513355,
Mob : 9880582331, 9845021552
Email:bharatsavla@yahoo.com

KOLHAPUR
Nirali Prakashan
New Mahadvar Road,
Kedar Plaza, 1st Floor Opp. IDBI Bank
Kolhapur 416 012, Maharashtra. Mob : 9855046155

CHENNAI
Pragati Books
9/1, Montieth Road, Behind Taas Mahal, Egmore,
Chennai 600008 Tamil Nadu, Tel : (044) 6518 3535,
Mob : 94440 01782 / 98450 21552 / 98805 82331, Email : bharatsavla@yahoo.com

RETAIL OUTLETS
PUNE

Pragati Book Centre
157, Budhwar Peth, Opp. Ratan Talkies,
Pune 411002, Maharashtra
Tel : (020) 2445 8887 / 6602 2707, Fax : (020) 2445 8887

Pragati Book Centre
676/B, Budhwar Peth, Opp. Jogeshwari Mandir,
Pune 411002, Maharashtra
Tel : (020) 6601 7784 / 6602 0855

Pragati Book Centre
Amber Chamber, 28/A, Budhwar Peth,
Appa Balwant Chowk, Pune : 411002, Maharashtra,
Tel : (020) 20240335 / 66281669
Email : pbcpune@pragationline.com

PBC Book Sellers & Stationers
152, Budhwar Peth, Pune 411002, Maharashtra
Tel : (020) 2445 2254 / 6609 2463

MUMBAI
Pragati Book Corner
Indira Niwas, 111 - A, Bhavani Shankar Road, Dadar (W), Mumbai 400028, Maharashtra
Tel : (022) 2422 3526 / 6662 5254, Email : pbcmumbai@pragationline.com

www.pragationline.com　　　　　　　　　　　　　　　　　　　　　　info@pragationline.com

Preface ...

Corporate form of business is the most popular form of business organisation due to the advantages associated with it. Although principles of finance are the same for all types of businesses, it has a different approach for a corporate, due to the separation of ownership and management, which gives rise to conflict of interest between the owners and managers. Hence there are regulations in place for the protection of interest of the stakeholders of a company. Corporate Finance lays stress on these aspects of corporate form of business. "Regulations" related to Corporate Governance is an example.

This book is compiled strictly according to the revised syllabus of Savitribai Phule Pune University. Exercise is given at the end of each chapter. Students are advised to answer those questions in order to test their knowledge.

I am extremely thankful to Mr Dineshbhai Furia and Mr. Jignesh Furia for entrusting me with the work of compiling the book. I am also thankful to the editorial team of Nirali Prakashan for their valuable help.

Wishing the students good luck.

Meera Govindaraj

Syllabus ...

Number of Sessions

1. **Goals and Governance of the Firm:** (7 + 2)

    Corporate Investment and Financial Decisions (Investment Decisions and Financing Decisions), Goals of the Corporations.

2. **Business Valuation** (7 + 2)

    Concept of Valuation, Different Concept of Value - Book-Value, Market Value, Intrinsic Value, Liquidation Value, Replacement Value, Salvage Value and Fair Value. Major approaches to Valuation of Business - Asset Based, Earning Based, Market Value Based Fair Value Based. EVA and MVA.

3. **Corporate Value Based Management System** (7 + 2)

    Shareholders Value, Concept and Features of Value Based Management, Need for Value Based Management, Need, Benefits and Approaches of Value Based Management System **Corporate Governance:** Concept of Corporate Governance, Criteria for Good Corporate Governance, Corporate Governance in India, Corporate Governance (Clause 49 Listing Agreement), Models of Corporate Governance.

4. **Dividend Decisions** (7 + 2)

    Meaning, Types of Dividend, Important Considerations in Dividend Policy, Theories on Dividend Policies (Walter's Approach, Gordon's Approach and Modigliani-Miller Approach)

5. **Corporate Restructuring** (7 + 2)

    Concept of Restructuring, Reasons for Restructuring, Broad Areas of Restructuring, Techniques of Corporate Restructuring – Expansion Technique, Divestment Technique, Other Techniques, Strategies for Restructuring.

- Numerical Problems will be asked on the following topics only - Business Valuation and Dividend Decisions. The weightage of theory questions will be 60% and numerical problems 40%.

***

Contents ...

1. Goals and Governance of the Firm — 1.1 - 1.22

2. Business Valuation — 2.1 - 2.26

3. Corporate Value Based Management System — 3.1 - 3.38

4. Dividend Decisions — 4.1 - 4.32

5. Corporate Restructuring — 5.1 - 5.18

6. Case Study — C.1 - C.5

***

Chapter 1...

Goals and Governance of the Firm

Contents ...
1.1 Introduction
1.2 Corporation
    1.2.1 Meaning of Corporation
    1.2.2 Goals of the Corporation
    1.2.3 Shareholder Wealth Maximisation (SWM)
    1.2.4 Corporate Wealth Maximisation (CWM)
1.3 Corporate Philanthropy
1.4 Corporate Investment and Financing Decisions
    1.4.1 Investment Decisions
    1.4.2 Financing Decisions
- Points to Remember
- Questions for Discussion
- Multiple Choice Questions
- Project Questions

Learning Objectives...
- To understand the goals and governance rules of a firm
- To study the corporate investment decisions of a firm
- To know the financial decisions of a firm

1.1 Introduction

The objective of a business firm is to maximise profits. There are firms which have other objectives too such as increasing the number of employees, serving the poor, increasing the market share, customer satisfaction etc. Even in cases when the objectives are other than 'maximisation of profits', the firm has to make profits in order to survive, for loss making organisations eventually close down.

Suppose the objective of an organisation is to generate employment. The firm must earn sufficient income to meet the increasing cost of employees arising out of new employment and due to the cost of retention of existing employees. A firm which is not earning profits will not be able to generate new jobs.

1.2 Corporation

1.2.1 Meaning of Corporation

A corporation is a legal entity separate from the members owning it. It is created by law and is dissolved by law. The members collectively own it by contributing to the capital of the corporate. The number of members is large. The day to day management of the business is carried on by the Board of Directors appointed by the shareholders of the company. The 'Board of Directors', who manages a company form of business, is a trustee of the owners. Assets are purchased out of the funds of the stockholders and business is conducted on behalf of the large number of owners.

1.2.2 Goals of the Corporation

The primary goal of a business corporation is to earn profits for the owners. Corporate goal setting is the most important management activity. It is the starting point of all business activity, and all activities revolve around the goals of the organisation. The various goals can be:

(i) Profit maximisation
(ii) Sales volume maximisation
(iii) Sales revenue maximisation
(iv) Survival in the market
(v) Increase shareholder value
(vi) Increase market share of the products of the company
(vii) Stable dividend payout
(viii) Price stability
(ix) Customer satisfaction
(x) High quality products and services
(xi) Ethical goals
(xii) Stakeholder or corporate wealth maximisation

A company can adopt multiple objectives. There is a realisation that companies should aim at stakeholder value maximisation for the long run survival and profit making. Stakeholders include – shareholders, debenture holders, creditors, customers, lenders, employees and the society. Big businesses have adopted philanthropy along with financial goals.

Whatever may be the goals of an organisation, profit making is important to the survival of a business. Further it is this goal, for which a business comes into being. Loss making organisations cannot pursue philanthropy goals. Actually most of the above listed goals take a firm to profit maximisation in the long run. For example customer satisfaction, high quality of goods and services, employee satisfaction etc., eventually make a firm earn goodwill and profit. Thus earning money becomes a by-product of these goals. Out of the various goals mentioned, two goals are dealt with in detail – Shareholder Wealth Maximisation (SWM), Corporate Wealth Maximisation (CWM).

1.2.3 Shareholder Wealth Maximisation (SWM)

A firm should strive to maximise the return to its shareholders for a given risk. Shareholder return consist of: (i) Dividend on share, (ii) Capital gains in the form of increase in the market price of shares. Alternatively, the firm should minimise the risk to shareholders for a given rate of return.

Assumptions

SWM model is based on the following assumptions:

(i) Stock market is efficient, in the sense it discounts or captures all the expected 'return and risk' perceived by investors. Hence the share price appearing at the stock exchange is correct.

(ii) It quickly incorporates the new information related to the company, into the share price.

(iii) Share price are the basis for allocation of capital in the economy. This means highest amount of capital flows into the company whose shares are traded at high price in the stock market.

(iv) Risk is universal truth. It is defined as the additional risk the **firm's** shares bring to an otherwise diversified **portfolio.** Investors can avoid the operational risk of firm by **diversification.** The risk of individual security in the portfolio of the investor should not bother the management of a company, unless it increases the chances of bankruptcy. Systematic risk, the risk of market in general, cannot be eliminated. That means the share price will be a function of the stock market.

1.2.4 Corporate Wealth Maximisation (CWM)

In contrast to the shareholder wealth maximisation model, the corporation's objective should be to maximise the wealth of the stakeholders or the interested groups associated with the corporate, such as – management, labour, local community, suppliers, creditors, and even the government. The corporate wealth is not just restricted to financial wealth, such as cash, marketable securities etc. It includes the firm's technical market and human resources besides conventional financial report, the firm's market position as well as the knowledge and skill of its employees in technology, manufacturing process, marketing and administration of the enterprise. A corporation can maximise its wealth by maximising the value of the company and by aligning the interest of the stakeholders into the system in such a way that the interest of the stakeholder and the corporate wealth maximisation are tied together. For example employee incentive and bonus plans should be aligned to the increase in the value of the firm.

Assumptions: CWM is based on the following assumptions:

(i) It assumes that loyal shareholders should influence the company strategy and not the transient portfolio investor.

(ii) It assumes that the total risk i.e., sum of operational and financial risk does not matter. Rather the objective to generate earnings and dividends over the long run with as much certainty as possible should be the corporate goal.

1.3 Corporate Philanthropy

Corporate philanthropy is the act of a corporation aiming at promoting the welfare of others, generally through charitable acts. It is more than just a donation. It is an effort undertaken by businesses to improve human welfare. Wealthy promoters or owners of businesses establish foundations to facilitate their philanthropic efforts.

Bill Gates and his wife Melinda established the 'Bill and Melinda Gates Foundation' to support global development and global health programmes.

Ford Foundation focuses on strengthening democracy, improving economic opportunity and advancing education.

Narayana Hrudayalaya (NH), now known as Narayana Health founded in 2000 by Devi Shetty is a multi-speciality hospital chain in India headquartered in Bengaluru. It is known as a low cost and high quality Indian health care service provider. The unique business model has become a global health care and Harvard Business School case study. It is among the largest telemedicine networks.

It has been experienced by many businessmen that the philanthropy goal is the ultimate. It requires less work to increase the sales and profits of the business. It is possible for firms to provide goods and services to the poorest of the poor at affordable prices and still make profits. Still lots of studies are to be conducted in this area.

1.4 Corporate Investment and Financing Decisions

The two important aspects of corporate finance are investment decisions and financing decisions. The answers to questions, such as, how much, in which assets, and when to invest relates to investment decisions and from where, how much and when to raise finance required for investment in the business relates to financing decisions.

Business firms need real assets such as machinery, building, furniture, equipment, material etc. to produce goods and services. The decision regarding the 'kind of assets' to be acquired, is the investment decision. For acquiring the asset, businesses need finance. The decision regarding the source of finance is the financing decision. Thus investment decisions are those that are meant to acquire **real assets** for the firm, which are used by the firm to provide goods and services. On the other hand firms issue **financial assets** like shares, bonds, debentures or take bank loans to finance its investment in real assets.

1.4.1 Investment Decisions

Assets required by a firm can be grouped into:
(i) Fixed assets; and
(ii) Current assets.

Fixed assets are acquired for long-term use. Examples are plant and machinery, furniture, equipment etc. The amount of money invested in the fixed asset is called fixed capital. It is also called as sunk capital as the money invested in it cannot be easily recovered. If decisions regarding the acquisition of a fixed asset go wrong, the firm will not only lose the money invested in it but will also end up risking its future profit earning capacity.

Current assets are meant for short-term use. These assets are either converted into finished goods meant for sale or get used up in the process of production, or are convertible into cash within a short period of time or are already in liquid form. Examples are – stock of raw materials, book debts, cash and bank balances. The fund invested in these assets is called 'working capital' or floating capital.

A. Capital Budgeting Decisions

Capital budgeting decisions involve commitment of funds to long-term assets or fixed assets of the firm. The amount involved is huge, and these decisions are irreversible. Hence if the decision for acquisition of a fixed asset goes against the goal of the organisation, the consequences have to be borne by the firm for a long time.

In the words of **John Hampton,** "Capital budgeting describes the firm's formal planning process for the acquisition and investment of capital and results in a capital budget that is the firm's formal plan for the expenditure of money to purchase fixed assets".

Significance of Capital Budgeting Decisions

Capital budgeting is an important decision due to the following reasons:

1. **Commitment of Huge Sums of Money**: It involves huge sums of money for a considerable period of time. Once a decision regarding investment is taken, funds will have to be committed either once for all or over a period of time. It makes the firm less flexible.

2. **Irreversible:** Capital budgeting decisions are almost irreversible. Once investment is made, it is not possible to withdraw the funds committed into the projects without loss.
3. **Long Term Effect on Profitability:** Investment decisions are based on future sales/income forecast. If the expected sale is not generated by the project, then there will be a long-term adverse effect on the profitability of the firm. Hence these decisions involve lot of risk.
4. **Basis of Financing Decisions:** The amount, source and timing of finance for the selected project are based on the capital budgeting decision.

Kinds of Capital Budgeting Decisions

The capital budgeting decisions can be of the following four kinds:

1. **Mutually Exclusive Decisions:** While choosing the best out of the available investment opportunities, one can be chosen to the exclusion of the other available alternatives. Out of two alternatives, only one can be chosen, the other is rejected. For example the company has two alternatives – to purchase Machinery X or Machinery Y. Under the capital budgeting process, the two machines' expected returns will be weighed against each other and the one with higher expected returns will be chosen. If X is chosen Y is rejected.
2. **Independent Projects:** When a company has a proposal for investment, it can either accept or reject it, based on standard criteria. The acceptance or rejection of the proposal is independent of any other investment by the company. For example company wants to know if Project X would increase the profitability of the company. Capital budgeting techniques would be applied and it would be found out if the project would generate profits. The project would be accepted if it fits in the requirement of the company or else would be rejected. The decision of acceptance or rejection of the project does not result in automatic acceptance or rejection of any other investment proposal.
3. **Replacement Decisions:** As the name suggests, these decisions involve replacement of an older asset which still has working life. A cost benefit analysis is done and a decision, about replacement or continuation of the asset, is taken.
4. **Capital Rationing Decision:** When fund available to the firm is less, then capital rationing decision helps the organisation in spending the funds on different requirements on the basis of priority. All the proposals are ranked in the order of priority and fund is allocated in the same order, till the available money is exhausted.

Methods of Evaluation of Investment Decisions

Techniques of evaluation of investment decisions can be grouped into two categories:

(i) Traditional methods i.e., the methods that do not use present value of money;

(ii) Discounted cash flow techniques, which use present value of money.

I. Traditional Methods: Under the Traditional methods the two important techniques are:

1. Payback Period: This method helps to calculate the period within which a firm can recover its investment in the project, out of the cash flow generated by the project. Earlier the recovery better is the project. This method is important for those firms that face liquidity problems and also in cases where it is difficult to forecast the expected cash inflow beyond a short period of time.

The best advantage of the technique is it is easy to calculate. Limitation of the technique includes:

(i) Time value of money is ignored; investment is made in the first year, whereas cash inflows are generated in the future years, when the value of money is lower. The inflows and outflows of cash are not comparable.

(ii) Post payback period cash inflow is as much important as the payback period.

(iii) It completely ignores the profitability aspect of project and concentrates on cash inflow alone.

2. Average Rate of Return (ARR): This method makes use of profitability of the projects rather than cash inflows. It is the expression of the "percentage return on investment" expected over the lifetime of the asset. The average profit is divided by the average investment and the ratio is multiplied with 100 to calculate percentage of return on the investment. Higher the percentage better is the project. It is an easy method but suffers from the same limitation of payback period, so far as 'time value' of money is concerned. Further, the method ignores cash flows which are more important for decision-making. Since the method considers average investment and average returns, the actual size and returns of different proposals are not considered.

II. Discounted Cash Flow Techniques: These techniques make use of present value of money for decision-making. An amount of money available today is more valuable than the same amount receivable after a year's time due to two reasons – interest involved and opportunity of income. The rate of interest, the uncertainty associated with future, the opportunity cost, all are considered while calculating the rate of discount for the future cash flows. If 10% is the discount factor, then every year 10% is the reduction in the value of money. Present value of rupee 1 is calculated by applying the following formula:

Present value of one rupee = $\dfrac{1}{(1+r)^n}$

Where 'r' is the rate of discount divided by 100 and 'n' is number of years.

The future cash flows are multiplied with the present value of rupee one for the selected discount rate, to obtain present value of cash flows.

Following are the important methods which use present value of money:

1. **Discounted Payback Period**: This method is the payback period calculation with a difference that the cash inflows and outflows are converted into present values before calculation of the period. It has all the advantages of traditional payback period technique with the added advantage of use of present value of money.

2. **Net Present Value Method (NPV):** It is defined as the difference between the present value of future cash inflows from a project and the present value of cash outflow for the project. The future cash inflows are discounted at a specified rate to get the present values of future cash inflow. The total of present values of cash inflow is compared with the present value of cash outflow for the project. If the cash inflows have higher value than cash outflows, then the project is said to have positive NPV and hence is selected. A project having negative NPV i.e., the present value of cash outflow beat out the present values of cash inflows, the project is rejected. In case where more than one alternative shows positive NPV, then the project with highest NPV is selected. This method is considered the best method of capital budgeting.

3. **Present Value Index:** It is a modification of NPV method. The present value of cash inflow is divided by the present value of cash outflow. If the quotient is more than one, the project is selected and if the answer is less than one, the project is rejected.

4. **Internal Rate of Return (IRR):** Internal rate is the rate at which the discounted cash inflow is equal to the discounted cash outflow. A project is accepted if the IRR is more than or equal to the required rate of return or the cut off rate of the firm. In case more than one alternative meets the criteria then the one with higher IRR is selected. It has all the advantages of NPV method. It is comparatively difficult to compute IRR.

B. **Working Capital Management:**

Working capital refers to the investment made by a firm in its current assets. These assets are either consumed in the process of production or are converted into cash within a short span of time. Examples are stock of finished goods, stock of raw material, debtors, accounts receivable, cash, readily marketable securities, etc. The decision regarding the amount to be invested in the current asset is an important aspect of working capital management.

A shortage in the working capital can cause stoppage in production and an excess amount in the same can reduce the profitability of the firm by increasing the holding cost of the asset and opportunity cost. A trade off between liquidity and profitability is desirable. Higher the liquidity, lower the risk and lower the profitability. Lower the liquidity, higher the risk and higher the profit (due to less blocking of funds).

Large amount of investment in current asset reduces the risk associated with the following:

(i) Stoppage of production due to non-availability of material, non-payment of power bill, or non-payment of wages etc.
(ii) Inability to meet short-term obligations like various outstanding payment including tax dues, debentures meant to be redeemed, payment of interest on loans etc.
(iii) Inability to meet market demand due to fall in production.

But it increases the cost associated with it. An excess investment in current asset increases the amount blocked in these assets and causes loss of interest, opportunity and increases maintenance cost of stock and stores. The increase in the cost reduces the profitability of the firm. Hence a firm has to strike a balance between cost and benefits of liquidity. What is the optimum amount of investment in working capital? There are a large number of factors that determine the working capital requirement of a firm.

Factors Determining Working Capital Requirement

1. **Length of the Working Capital Cycle:** Time taken by the raw material to get converted into cash is the working capital cycle. Longer the time it takes for the stocks to be converted into working capital, larger will be the requirement of working capital as during the period the firm would need funds to carry on its operations. If the time of the cycle is short, the working capital requirement will be less, as the firm gets the cash quickly out of its business operations.
2. **Scale of Operation:** Larger the scale of operation, greater will be the need for working capital and vice-versa. This is simply because the firm would need more money to invest in the purchase of stock, stores and to meet the day to day expenses etc.
3. **Nature of Business:** A firm that provides 'service' will require lesser amount of working capital, when compared to trading and manufacturing organisations. The important reason for it is the cost involved in purchasing and maintaining inventories.
4. **Dividend Policy:** Companies following high dividend payout ratio, require more cash to pay the dividends. If a small portion of profits is distributed as dividend, then the cash required is less, hence working capital requirement will be less.

5. **Credit Policy of the Firm:** The credit policy of the firm for debt collection and payment is another important determinant of working capital requirement. Longer the debt collection period, greater will be the need for working capital and vice-versa. Shorter the payment period greater will be the need for working capital.
6. **Growth of Firm:** During the growth period, a firm requires more working capital.
7. **Supply of Raw Material, Spare Parts, and Stores etc.:** If the supply of raw material, stores and spare parts is regular, then a firm need not keep large stocks of these to meet its requirements. In such a case the working capital requirement will be less. On the other hand if the firm needs a material that has to be imported or is scarce in supply or is not timely available, then large quantities of stocks will have to be bought, which will increase the working capital requirement.

1.4.2 Financing Decisions

Investment decision is broadly concerned with determination of asset mix or the composition of the assets of a firm. Financing decision, on the other hand, is concerned with obtaining the right amount of finance, from the right source at the right time to make investment in assets of the firm. Investment decisions relates to the asset side of the Balance Sheet whereas financing decision is concerned with the liability side of the Balance Sheet. The following questions need to be answered:

(i) What is the amount of funds to be raised?
(ii) Which source of raising finance is suitable?
(iii) What is the timing of raising finance?
(iv) What should be the proportion of owned fund and borrowed fund in the capital structure of the company?

All these decisions need to be taken at a time. These are interlinked. The total amount required has to be divided as per the source of finance and as per the timing. The selection of source of finance must match with the optimal capital structure of the firm. Thus the most important aspect of financing decision is the capital structure decision. Capital structure theories help in decision-making.

Capital Structure Theories

Capital structure theories explain the theoretical relationship between cost of capital and the value of a firm. The object of any firm is to reduce cost of capital and maximise the value of the firm. Important theories are:

(a) **Net Income Approach:** According to the theory capital structure affects the cost of capital and value of a firm. Hence firms must find out the optimal capital structure for them. The explanation given is – as the use of debt in the capital of a firm is increased, the overall cost of capital falls. The cost of debt and that of equity remains constant with the increase in debt-equity ratio. The weighted average cost of capital decreases with the increase in the proportion of debt as debt is less costly than equity. With the fall in the overall cost of capital the value of the firm increases.

(b) Net Operating Income Approach: This method is based on the change in the expectation of equity shareholder, with the increase in the debt-equity ratio. When a firm finances its business activity through debt, the profit earned over and above the cost of debt is added to the earnings of the owners, resulting in an increase in the EPS. Since shareholders are aware of this phenomenon, their expectation and hence cost of equity increases with the increase in the debt proportion. Thus the benefit is washed away due to increase in the cost of equity. Hence, according to the approach, there is no optimal capital structure.

(c) MM Approach: According to the approach choice of capital structure does not affect the value of a firm, which is the result of efficiency of a firm. Therefore there is no best capital structure. The explanation given by them is the 'arbitrage process'. Companies with similar size of activity, profit and risk cannot have different values. If at all values are different at one particular time, then correction will take place due to the arbitrage process. The investors of a highly valued firm would sell their investment and use the funds to buy more number of shares of the company with lower value and thus earn profit as well as high income. This process will continue till values of the two firms are brought at same level.

(d) Traditional Approach: This approach is midway between the NI and NOI approaches. According to this approach, a firm can increase its value and reduce cost of capital by a judicious combination of debt and equity. However, beyond a certain point, the risk to the investors, as well as, to the creditors would increase. The increased cost would reduce the value of the firm. The point is the optimal mix of debt and equity.

EBIT-EPS Relation: Theories of capital structure help in understanding the relationship between the capital structure of a company and value of a firm. Every firm has to plan its capital structure based on the facts and circumstances of the firm. One of the most important techniques to design appropriate capital structure is the EBIT-EPS analysis. It essentially involves comparison of the alternative methods of finance available to the firm. That alternative capital structure that gives maximum EPS for a given level of EBIT shall be chosen. Or the alternative selected should give maximum market price per share (Market price = EPS x P/E). The technique makes use of indifference point. It is that level of EBIT at which EPS is same for different financial plan (capital structure). If the expected level of EBIT is beyond the indifference point then the use of debt will result in higher EPS and if the EBIT expected from the finance is expected to be less than that at the indifference point then the company should not use debt. Use of equity would, in such situations increase the EPS.

The indifference point is obtained by plotting the EBIT on the 'X' axis and corresponding EPS on the 'Y' axis. The points are joined for each of the financial plans. Wherever the lines interact, is the point of indifference. At this point debt-equity ratio does not matter. Beyond the point of indifference, use of debt will bring higher EPS and below the point use of equity gives higher EPS. Mathematically we can use the following formula to find that level of EBIT where the company can use any combination of different source of finance without affecting the EPS.

1. **Equity and debentures are the alternative source of finance**

   $X(1 - t)/N_1 = [(X - I)(1 - t)/N_2]$

2. **Equity shares and Preference shares**

   $X(1 - t)/N_1 = [(X - I) - D_p]/N_3$

3. **Equity versus Preference shares and Debentures**

   $X(1 - t)/N_1 = [(X - I)(1 - t) - D_p]/N_4$

   Where X is the EBIT, which is to be found out

   N_1 is the number of equity shares to be issued as per plan 1

   N_2 is the number of equity shares to be issued as per plan 2

   Similarly N_3 and N_4 respectively are the number of equity shares to be issued under plans 3 and 4 respectively.

   $(1 - t)$ is 1 minus rate of tax divided by 100

   D_p = dividend on preference share

Weighted Average Cost of Capital (WACC)

Weighted average cost of capital is the average cost of all the sources of capital used by the firm. Value of the firm is maximised by minimising the weighted average cost of capital. A company needs to analyse the impact of tapping a particular source of funds, on the WACC of the firm. WACC is found out by adding the product of proportion of every source of capital with its respective after tax cost.

The various **sources of finance** available to a firm can be broadly grouped under two categories: (a) Ownership capital, (b) Borrowed capital.

Ownership funds can be raised by a company by rights issue of fresh issue of shares. When rights are issued, there is no dilution of control, nor extra burden on the income of the company as dividend is an appropriation of profit. Shares can be Equity shares or Preference shares. Preference shareholders have a preferential treatment with regard to dividend payment and return of capital on liquidation when compared to equity shareholders. The dividend on the preference share is predetermined. The equity shareholders have claim over the residual profits of the company, after the payment of dues on borrowed capital, income tax and preference dividend.

Borrowed funds can be in the form of loans from banks and financial institutions, debenture and public deposit. Interest is to be paid by the company which is tax deductible, and the principal amount has to be repaid within the period agreed. Each source has its own advantages and limitations.

Buy or Lease: A firm can buy the fixed assets, or may take on lease. If it decides to buy it can use one or more of the various sources of finance in the category of owned funds and debt funds. Instead of making purchase of fixed assets a company can go for leasing.

Lease is one of the methods of financing fixed assets of an enterprise. A firm which has an inadequacy of funds or does not want to commit its funds on the fixed asset may adopt lease. Lease is an agreement entered into with the owner of fixed asset to use the asset for a fixed period of time against a periodical payment. After the expiry of the period the lease agreement may be renewed or the asset may be purchased by the lessee.

Characteristic Features of Leasing
1. It is a contract between lessor and lessee.
2. The contract gives a right to the lessee to use an asset in return for a payment.
3. The contract is for a limited period of time but can be renewed for a further period.
4. Lessor is the owner of the asset.
5. On the expiry of the period of lease, the lessor may sell the asset to the lessee or any other party.

Types of Lease

Leases are classified into different types based on the variations in the elements of the lease agreement. Most popular classification of lease is – financial lease and operating lease. Apart from these, there are sale and lease back, direct lease, single investor lease and leveraged lease, and domestic and international lease. The variations can be in certain elements of the lease agreement as follows:
  (i) the degree of ownership risk and rewards transferred to the lessee;
  (ii) location of the lessor, lessee and the equipment supplier;
  (iii) number of parties involved.

I. Financial Lease and Operating Lease

Financial lease is also called as Full Payout lease. Under this kind of lease agreement, the lessor transfers substantially all the risks and rewards associated with the asset to the lessee.

The ownership gets transferred at the end of the economic life of the asset. Lease term is spread over the major part of the asset's life. It has the following features:

(i) It is for a long period of time, normally equal to the expected useful life of the asset;
(ii) It is not cancellable;
(iii) Usually the maintenance of the property, property taxes and insurance is provided by the lessee;
(iv) The risk and rewards associated with the lease is transferred to the lessee;
(v) The burden of obsolescence falls on the lessee.

The companies that frequently update or replace equipment and want to use equipment for less than its economic life may not like to go for financial lease. Operating lease does not run for full economic life of the asset, and the lessee is not liable for financing its full value. Lessor carries the risk associated with the asset. Maintenance, property taxes and insurance are usually provided by the lessor. Thus along with the right to use the property, the lessee obtains some services also. The main features of operating lease are:

- Normally leasing of the assets is the regular business of the lessor;
- In most of the cases, the lease is cancellable at the instance of the lessor;
- The lease period is relatively short, not exceeding 2 or 3 years;
- The capital cost of the asset cannot be recovered from one such lease of the asset as the lease period is short. Hence the lessor leases the property a number of times either to the same lessee or to another lessee;
- The maintenance of the property, the payment of property taxes and insurance usually falls on the lessor.
- The risk of obsolescence falls on the lessor.

II. Sale and Lease Back

Under this method of lease the owner of an asset sells the asset to another person without giving away the possession of the asset. The purchaser of the asset now becomes owner of the property and enters into a lease agreement with the vendor of the asset who becomes the lessee after the contract of lease. The original owner pays rentals for use of the asset to the current owner of the asset. Thus under sale and lease back seller becomes the lessee and the buyer becomes the lessor of the property.

III. Leveraged Lease

Under leveraged leasing arrangement, the lessor borrows funds to buy the asset meant to be leased out. Around 80% of the cost of the asset is borrowed from a third party on the security of the asset. The asset is leased out in the regular manner. The lease rental received from the lessee is used to repay the loan.

IV. Direct Leasing

Under direct leasing, a firm acquires the right to use an asset from the manufacturer directly. The ownership of the asset remains with the manufacturer.

V. Big Ticket Leasing

This method of leasing is more popular for very expensive assets such as construction equipment, sophisticated computer system, heavy machinery etc. The cost of asset is so huge that it may not be possible for one lessor to provide the asset on lease. Two or more lessor companies join hands in leasing. The asset may be funded by the lessors themselves or they might be financed partly by the lessors, and partly lender of it and the rest may be financed with borrowed funds.

VI. Cross-border Leasing

When the lessor and the lessee belong to different countries the leasing arrangement is called cross-border leasing.

VII. In-house Leasing

When a group of companies promote a leasing company for the benefit of the companies in the group, the company is called the 'in-house leasing company'. In-house leasing company provides a lot of benefits to the group companies.

VIII. On the basis of the Terms of Payment

- **Balloon Rental Leasing:** Here the initial rent amounts are lower and the rent amount increases during the later period of the lease.
- **Step Rental Leasing:** Under this arrangement the rent amount is not fixed for the whole of the period of lease. It depends upon the size of income flow of the lessee.
- **Front Heavy Type Leasing:** According to this arrangement, larger rentals are collected in the initial period of the lease and lower amount of rent is charged during the later part of the lease.
- **Skipped Payment Leasing:** Under this arrangement, a rental of certain periods, when the equipment is not functioning, is skipped.
- **Trial Period Leasing:** Under this arrangement the lessee is allowed to take lease on a trial basis for sometime before deciding to take the asset on lease.

Advantages of Leasing

(i) Lessee gets the benefit of use of the asset without making any payment towards the purchase of the asset. Funds thus saved can be used for working capital requirements.

(ii) The lease agreement can be made to suit the needs of the lessee and lessor. There is a lot of flexibility.

(iii) It is a cheaper source of financing when compared to debt financing.

(iv) The rent paid is chargeable to the profit and loss account of the lessee. Thus the lessee gets tax advantage.

Disadvantages of Leasing

(i) The lessor usually charges higher rate of interest than the rate he pays on borrowings.

(ii) The residual value of the asset may accrue to the lessor.

Risk

Risk is a possibility of financial loss (either in absolute terms or relative to expectations) that is inseparable from the opportunity for financial gain. Some of the major categories of risk are:

- Market risk
- Credit risk
- Liquidity risk; and
- Operational risk

Market risk arises from changes in prices in financial markets. Credit risk relates to the failure of payment. Liquidity risk is that of running out of cash to meet day-to-day obligations. Operational risk is a catch-all category that covers a firm's internal systems and processes, as well as external events.

(I) Business Risk

Business risk is the risk that is inherent in the business operations of a company. It is caused by factors other than factors concerned with capital structure. Some of these factors are detailed below:

(a) Company related factors:
   (i) Labour relation
   (ii) Managerial competence
   (iii) Competitive position
   (iv) Asset structures etc.

(b) Industry related factors:
   (i) Growth prospects of the industry
   (ii) Trade unions

(c) Economic factors:
   (i) Rate of inflation
   (ii) Recession
   (iii) Devaluation
   (iv) Government policy

Measurement of Business Risk

One of the widely used methods of measurement of business risk is by 'coefficient of variation' of the net operating income before for (EBIT). It is the ratio of standard deviation of expected value (mean).

$$C.V. = \frac{\sigma}{\bar{x}}$$

σ = Standard deviation of expected EBIT

$\bar{x}$ = Expected value that is the arithmetic mean of the EBIT

(II) Financial Risk

"Financial Risk is caused by the introduction of debt into the capital structure of a company". The use of debt in the capital structure of a company not only increases the return to the shareholders but also exposes them to the following risks:

1. Increased variability in the shareholders earnings.
2. The threat of insolvency.

<ol>
<li>Consumer goods industries face fluctuations in sales. A company with sales fluctuations cannot employ more debt as the earnings of the shareholders will vary. Even a small percentage change in sales can cause a dramatic change in the earning per share. So shareholders of such companies perceive a high degree of risk.</li>
<li>During adverse operating conditions when costs increase, companies with usable sales may suffer from liquidity crisis. It may find it tough to meet its obligations in time.</li>
</ol>

Measurement of Financial Risk

Financial risk can be measured with the help of the following:

(a) Debt-Equity Ratio: This ratio expresses the ratio between the long-term debt and owners funds. Long-term debts include Debenture and Term loans. Equity includes the paid-up share to capital plus reserves and surpluses minus operating losses.

$$\text{Debt-equity ratio} = \frac{\text{Long term debt}}{\text{Net worth / Equity}}$$

(b) Debt-Capital Ratio: This ratio expresses the relationship between the long-term debt and the total capital of the company. Total capital includes debt as well as net worth. The formula is stated below:

$$\text{Debt-equity ratio} = \frac{\text{Long term debt}}{\text{Total capital employed}}$$

(c) **Interest Coverage Ratio:** This ratio indicates the number of times the fixed interest payable is covered by the earnings of the company. It is computed by applying the following formula:

$$\text{Interest Coverage} = \frac{\text{EBIT}}{\text{Interest}}$$

This ratio is used to test the firm's debt-servicing capacity.

Financial risk is viewed as the probability of a company going insolvent due to its inability to meet interest obligations as and when they fall due. Financial risk unlike business risk is controllable. A company can change its financial risk by changing its capital structure.

Shareholder value is maximised by keeping the total risk at a low level. If financial risk is high operating risk should be low and vice-versa.

Time of Floatation

Financial planning involves the decision regarding the timing of floatation of a company's securities. In order to make capital issue successful, the right time must be determined. The timing is related to the economic conditions prevailing in the country. All economies face a simultaneous change in investment, employment, output and prices. These changes recur and are called trade cycles. The four phases of a business cycle are described as follows:

1. **Boom**

This is a period of high investment, high employment and large volume of output in the economy. The prices rise, there is lot of demand for funds and the rate of interest is very high.

2. **Recession**

This is a period of slowdown or fall in the rate of economic growth. This period is associated with falling levels of investment, rising unemployment and falling prices.

3. **Depression**

This is a period of severe recession. Economic activities are at their lowest. It is a period of crisis. Many business firms close down, resulting in unemployment. There is gloom everywhere.

4. **Recovery**

This is a period when the business activity shows signs of recovery since the piled up stocks of the depression period are completely sold and the businessmen look for funds to produce the basic minimum output. This slowly introduces activity gain.

The best time for floating securities is when business is booming and people are optimistic.

Conclusion: The essential difference between investment and financing decision is investment asset results in acquisition of real asset, whereas financing decision results in the acquisition of financial assets. Real assets are used to generate returns and there is a risk that the decision about acquisition of asset goes wrong and the expected return is not forthcoming. The cost associated with the financing asset is to be borne out of the returns.

Points to Remember

- **A corporation** is a legal entity separate from the members owning it. It is created by law and is dissolved by law.
- The various goals can be:
    1. Profit maximisation
    2. Sales volume maximisation
    3. Sales revenue maximisation
    4. Survival in the market
    5. Increase shareholder value
    6. Increase market share of the products of the company
    7. Stable dividend payout
    8. Price stability
    9. Customer satisfaction
    10. High Quality products and services
    11. Ethical goals
    12. Stakeholder or corporate wealth maximisation
- Corporate philanthropy is the act of a corporation aiming at promoting the welfare of others, generally through charitable acts.
- **Assets required by a firm can be grouped into:**
    1. Fixed assets; and
    2. Current assets.
- **Capital budgeting decisions** involve commitment of funds to long-term assets or fixed assets of the firm.
- **Investment decision** is broadly concerned with determination of asset mix or the composition of the assets of a firm.
- Financing decision is concerned with obtaining the right amount of finance, from the right source at the right time to make investment in assets of the firm.
- **Net Income Approach:** According to the theory capital structure affects the cost of capital and value of a firm.

- **Net Operating Income Approach**: This method is based on the change in the expectation of equity shareholder, with the increase in the debt-equity ratio.
- **MM Approach**: According to the approach choice of capital structure does not affect the value of a firm, which is the result of the efficiency of a firm. Therefore there is no best capital structure.
- **Traditional Approach**: This approach is midway between the NI and NOI approaches. According to this approach, a firm can increase its value and reduce cost of capital by a judicious combination of debt and equity.
- Weighted average cost of capital is the average cost of all the sources of capital used by the firm.
- The various **sources of finance** available to a firm can be broadly grouped under two categories – a. Ownership capital and b. Borrowed capital.
- Risk is a possibility of financial loss (either in absolute terms or relative to expectations) that is inseparable from the opportunity for financial gain.
- Some of the major categories of risk are:
1. Market risk
2. Credit risk
3. Liquidity risk; and
4. Operational risk.

Questions for Discussion

1. What is corporate philanthropy?
2. What are the assumptions underlying the shareholder wealth maximisation objective?
3. What are the assumptions of corporate wealth maximisation?
4. What is business risk? What are the types of risk?
5. Differentiate between investment decisions and financing decisions.
6. What is net present value?
7. What is capital budgeting? What are the techniques of capital budgeting?
8. What is meant by corporate goals? What are the various goals corporations have?
9. What is capital structure? Explain the various theories of capital structure.
10. What are operating lease and financial lease? What are the advantages of lease contracts?
11. Explain the types of lease agreements.
12. What is indifference point? How does it help in taking financing decisions? What are the methods of calculating the indifference point?

Multiple Choice Questions

1. A legal entity independent of its owners is ......
    - (a) firm
    - (b) business organisation
    - (c) corporation
    - (d) local bodies
2. Shareholder wealth maximisation is measured in terms of increase in ......
    - (a) EPS
    - (b) market value of the firm
    - (c) dividend and market value of the firm
    - (d) market price of the equity shares
3. Corporate wealth maximisation is the value maximisation for ......
    - (a) equity shareholders
    - (b) stakeholders
    - (c) employees
    - (d) shareholders as well as debt capital owners
4. The promotion of welfare of human by corporate is ......
    - (a) social service
    - (b) philosophy
    - (c) the work of NGOs
    - (d) corporate philanthropy
5. Leasing a machinery is an example of ......
    - (a) fixed asset
    - (b) investment decision
    - (c) financing decision
    - (d) capital budgeting decision
6. Net profit is the basis for the calculation of ......
    - (a) Average rate of return
    - (b) Net present value
    - (c) Internal rate of return
    - (d) Payback period
7. A decision of acceptance of an alternative, amounts to rejection of the other is ......
    - (a) independent decision
    - (b) mutually exclusive decision
    - (c) capital rationing decision
    - (d) replacement decision
8. The rate at which the discounted cash inflow is equal to the discounted cash outflow is ......
    - (a) IRR
    - (b) ARR
    - (c) discount rate
    - (d) payback period

9. Purchase of real asset is ......
   (a) financing decision
   (b) mutually exclusive decision
   (c) capital budgeting decision
   (d) investment decision

10. Arbitrage process is an explanation to ......
    (a) net income approach
    (b) net operating income approach
    (c) MM approach
    (d) both NOI and MM approaches

11. Indifference point is that amount of EBIT ......
    (a) below the point use of debt generates higher EPS
    (b) below the point use of owned capital gives higher EPS
    (c) above the point use of debt is desirable
    (d) the capital structure does not matter

ANSWERS

1. (c)	2. (c)	3. (b)	4. (d)	5. (c)	6. (a)	7. (b)	8. (a)
9. (d)	10. (c)	11. (d)					

Project Questions

1. Managers of companies face an impossible task because they cannot really increase the wealth of each and every shareholder. Because there are thousands of shareholders, it is impossible to find projects that allow the managers to meet the investment and consumption needs of every shareholder. As a consequence, managers should follow the rule that they should invest in projects that provide them with the best satisfaction and not consider the needs of investors. Do you agree? What investment rules should managers follow and why?

2. You were told by the management of ABC Limited that the company's goals are to maximise the company's assets. Is this consistent with maximising shareholder wealth?

Chapter 2...

Business Valuation

Contents ...
- 2.1 Business Valuation
    - 2.1.1 Concept of Valuation
    - 2.1.2 Different Concepts of Value
- 2.2 Major Approaches to Business Valuation
    - 2.2.1 Asset based Approach to Business Valuation
    - 2.2.2 Earnings Based Approach
    - 2.2.3 Market Value based Approach to Valuation
    - 2.2.4 Fair Value Method
    - 2.2.5 Market Value Added Method (MVA)
    - 2.2.6 Economic Value Added Method (EVA)
- Points to Remember
- Questions for Discussion
- Multiple Choice Questions
- Practical Problems

Learning Objectives...
- To understand the concept of business valuation
- To study the various concepts of value involving:
    1. Book Value
    2. Market Value
    3. Intrinsic Value
    4. Liquidation Value
    5. Replacement Value
    6. Salvage Value
    7. Fair Value
- To learn the various approaches to business valuation including:
    1. Asset based Valuation
    2. Earning based Valuation
    3. Market Value based Valuation
    4. Fair Value based valuation
    5. Economic value added (EVA)
    6. Market Value added (MVA)

2.1 Business Valuation

2.1.1 Concept of Valuation

The process of determining the worth or value of an asset or business is valuation. For example, stock analysts typically give a publicly traded company a valuation. Investment Bankers determine a valuation on a company using standard industry comparisons. Real estate has professionals called appraisers who put a valuation on a property.

Valuation is the process by which worth of an asset, business or a security is determined. The process is undertaken by a pre-determined purpose, using an appropriate method by the experts in the field.

Valuation of business requires a careful selection of method of valuation of assets for both tangible and intangible assets, fixed and current assets, existing liabilities and contingent liabilities, determination of future expected earnings or cash flows of the business, the capitalisation rate and P/E ratio, etc.

2.1.2 Different Concepts of Value

There are a number of methods used by finance managers for valuing a business. The most appropriate method is selected keeping in view the circumstances of each case.

The various concepts of valuation include:

1. Book Value: Book value refers to the amount at which the assets and liabilities appear in the books of the company; the value at which the assets may be shown in the Balance Sheet if it is prepared on the valuation day. Under the method fixed assets are shown at cost less depreciation, current assets at cost less provision for bad debts in the case of debtors and obsolescence in case of stocks and stores. The basic principle applied on the valuation under the method is – 'Going concern concept'. It means the value does not reflect the current realisable/market value. Fictitious assets like preliminary expenses, advertising expenses, underwriting commission not written off is not considered for ascertaining business value.

Book value is calculated by adding all the physical assets of a company (including land, buildings, computers, etc.) and subtracting out intangible assets (such as patents) and liabilities—including preferred stock, debt, and accounts payable. The value left after this calculation represents what is the intrinsic worth of the company.

Thus, book value is calculated as follows:

Book value = Total assets – Intangible assets – Liabilities

While book value represents the intrinsic net worth of a company, it is a helpful tool for investors wanting to determine if a company is underpriced or overpriced, which could indicate a potential time to buy or sell. For instance, value investors search for companies trading for prices at or below book value (indicating a price-to-book ratio of less than 1.0), which implies the shares are selling for less than the company's actual worth.

   2. **Market Value:** Under this method assets and liabilities are valued at market value. It is opposite to the book value method. This method can be used with respect to the tangible assets only. Intangible assets do not have market value.

The market value is the value or price for which a share currently trades in the marketplace, usually determined by the interaction of supply and demand for the share. Because the market value is based on the dynamics of supply and demand, which is often the result of speculative motives or sentiment, if often does not indicate the 'true or real' value of the share in the company.

   3. **Intrinsic Value:** It is also called as the economic value of an asset and is used in 'Capital Budgeting' decisions. It is based on discounted cash flows after tax expected to be generated by an asset. The discount rate is carefully selected. It is the rate of return expected by the equity shareholders of the company. It represents the maximum amount purchaser would be ready to pay.

This value is considered to be the 'real' value of a share, and is equivalent to the present value of all the asset's expected future cash flows discounted at the investor's appropriate risk-adjusted required rate of return. Intrinsic value represents an individual investor's own personal perception or interpretation of an asset's value. Intrinsic value may or may not equal market value, although in an efficient market they should be equal.

It is valuable to calculate the intrinsic value of a share because this would indicate whether the market price is currently under or overvalued.

The actual value of a company or an asset based on an underlying perception of its true value including all aspects of the business, in terms of both tangible and intangible factors, may or may not be the same as the current market value. Value investors use a variety of analytical techniques in order to estimate the intrinsic value of securities in hopes of finding investments where the true value of the investment exceeds its current market value.

For call options, this is the difference between the underlying stock's price and the strike price. For put options, it is the difference between the strike price and the underlying stock's price. In the case of both puts and calls, if the respective difference value is negative, the intrinsic value is given as zero.

   4. **Liquidation Value:** It represents the value at which an asset could be sold if business is discontinued. Liquidation value is lower compared to book value, market value and intrinsic value of an asset.

Liquidation value is the price of a company's tangible assets if it goes out of business and needs to be liquidated within a limited period of time. Liquidation value is typically lower than fair market value as is it allowed insufficient exposure to the investors in the open market. Intangible assets, including the intellectual properties, reputations and goodwill, are not included in liquidation value. If the company was to be sold rather than liquidated, then the price is called **going–concern value** which includes the liquidation value and the present value of its intangible assets.

Liquidation value can be defined as the estimated amount of money that could be received quickly through the sale of an asset or a company. Put another way, the liquidation value refers to the worth of the physical assets of a company as it steps out of business or if it was supposed to go out of business.

If a company was to be sold off instead of being liquidated, both liquidation value as well as the intangible assets would be taken into account to calculate the going-concern value of the company. Besides, liquidation value also refers to the cash value of a single asset.

Many investors, in the business of making money, want to know everything about a company, be it potential earnings or expected liquidation value. The liquidation value is generally used for the purpose of bankruptcies. Besides, lenders who are considering the application of a borrower also use liquidation value. In addition, bondholders are also interested in knowing the liquidation value as they are also considered as debtors to the company.

Liquidation value is estimated through assets like fixtures, real estate, equipment, and inventory owned by a company. Intangible assets like goodwill, business' intellectual property, and brand recognition are, however, not counted in the liquidation value of a company.

5. Replacement Value: It is value of an asset determined by ascertaining the cost of replacing the asset by purchasing a new asset of similar utility.

The term replacement cost or replacement value refers to the amount that an entity would have to pay to replace an asset at the present time, according to its current worth.

6. Salvage Value: It is the value of a fixed asset after its useful economic life. The asset is sold as scrap.

Salvage Value is the estimated value that an asset will realise upon its sale at the end of its useful life. The value is used in accounting to determine depreciation amounts and in the tax system to determine deductions. The value can be a best guess of the end value or can be determined by a regulatory body such as the IRS.

Salvage value is the projected value that an asset will realize on its sale at the end of its useful life. The price is used in accounting for deciding the depreciation amounts, and in the tax system to determine the deductions. *Salvage value* is the projected resale value of an asset at the close of its useful life. You deduct the salvage value from the cost of a fixed asset to decide the quantity of the asset price that you will depreciate. Thus, salvage value is solitarily used as a component of depreciation calculation.

If it is excessively difficult to govern a salvage value, or if it is expected to be negligible, then it is not necessary to include a salvage value in your depreciation calculations. Instead, simply depreciate the complete cost of the fixed asset over its useful life. You will then recognize the proceeds from the subsequent disposition of the asset as an advantage. Salvage value is not reduced to its present value. It is also known as residual value.

7. Fair Value: Technically it is calculated by averaging the three values of an asset – book value, market value and intrinsic value. Fair value is defined by the Internal Revenue Service of US as "the price at which property would change hands between a willing buyer and a willing seller when the former is not under any compulsion to buy and the latter is not under any compulsion to sell, both parties having reasonable knowledge of relevant facts."

2.2 Major Approaches to Business Valuation

The major approaches to valuation include:
1. Asset based Valuation
2. Earning based Valuation
3. Market Value based Valuation
4. Fair Value based Valuation
5. Economic Value Added (EVA)
6. Market Value Added (MVA)

2.2.1 Asset based Approach to Business Valuation

Under this method of business valuation, shareholder's net worth is calculated by deducting from the total value of assets, the amount of liabilities as well as the amount due to the preference shareholders. In order to find out the 'net asset' per equity share the net asset amount is divided by the number of equity shares.

The assets may be valued on the basis of the accounting principle of 'going concern' or on the basis of the value on winding up. The fixed assets will be taken at their book value. If an asset has lived its economic life then, it may be valued at scrap value or residual value. Current assets are to be valued at book value. It should be ensured that sufficient provision has been made for bad and doubtful debts and obsolescence of stocks and stores. Intangible asset like goodwill is valued by super profit method. Fictitious assets are not taken into consideration like preliminary expenses, advertising suspense account etc.

Corporate Finance — Business Valuation

While calculating liabilities, special attention has to be paid to contingent liability. If such liabilities have high chances of occurring, then those should also be added to the amount of liabilities. For the purpose of determining the equity shareholder's funds, the amount due to the preference shareholders, is also deducted.

Net Asset = Value of assets – Amount of liabilities – Amount due to preference shareholders

Net asset is then, divided by the number of equity share outstanding, in order to find out the net asset available for on equity share.

On liquidation of a company the assets are valued at liquidation value and not on book value. Liquidation value is less than book value.

Disadvantage:

The major disadvantage of this method of business valuation is that the value of business is based on the book value and not on the future profit or cash flow generating capacity of the firm.

Illustration 2.1

Balance Sheet of Slack Ltd. is given to you. You are required to calculate the price per equity share on the basis of net assets method.

Liabilities	₹	Assets	₹
Equity shares of ₹ 10	6,00,000	Land and building	16,00,000
Reserves	13,20,000	Plant and equipment	9,00,000
Dividend equalisation fund	2,00,000	Motor vehicles	1,20,000
Secured loan	8,00,000	Patents etc.	24,000
Staff welfare fund	20,000	Stock	4,00,000
Creditors	3,60,000	Debtors	3,00,000
Accrued expenses	1,00,000	Cash and bank balance	66,000
Proposed dividend	90,000	Deferred advertisement	80,000
	34,90,000		34,90,000

Net profits of the company after tax and interest for the last 5 years were – ₹ 1,80,000, ₹ 1,60,000, ₹ 2,10,000, ₹ 1,80,000, ₹ 2,00,000. The fixed assets have been valued by an independent expert as follows:

Land and Building ₹ 21,50,000, Plant and Equipment ₹ 9,60,000, Motor Vehicles ₹ 90,000.

The applicable price earnings ratio is 8. Compute the value per equity share of the company based on Net assets method.

Solution:

Computation of Net Asset

Particulars	₹
Computation of Net Asset	
Land and building	21,50,000
Plant and machinery	9,60,000
Motor vehicles	90,000
Intangibles	Nil
Stock	4,00,000
Debtors	3,00,000
Cash and bank	66,000
Total (a)	39,66,000
Secured loan	8,00,000
Creditors	3,60,000
Accrued expenses	1,00,000
Total (b)	12,60,000
Net assets (a-b)	27,06,000
Number of equity shares	60,000
Value of per equity share	45.10

2.2.2 Earnings Based Approach

This approach to business valuation removes the main drawback of the Net asset method. The business valuation under the approach is based on the future prospects of the business, rather than the value of assets possessed by it. Under the method the net earnings available to equity share holder or the present value of future cash flow expected to be generated by the firm is considered for valuation of business.

A. Earnings Capitalisation (as per Accounting) Method: Under the method future maintainable profit is determined and the amount so calculated is divided by an appropriate capitalisation rate, to arrive at the value of the business.

Maintainable profit is the average profit after tax adjusted for the following items:

    (i)   Additional income expected in the future years due to new product etc.;

    (ii) Profits or loss from the sale of fixed assets;

(iii) Loss due to theft, fire or natural calamities, strikes, lock-outs;
(iv) Expenditure on voluntary retirement;
(v) Any other item which is extraordinary in nature and is not expected to occur in the future years.

Capitalisation rate is the rate of earning expected by investors. Businesses exposed to higher risk have a higher capitalisation rate than firms with low risk.

Illustration 2.2: Super Tech Ltd. earned a profit of ₹ 4,78,000 after tax and after preference dividend. The capital structure of the company consisted of

	₹
1,00,000 Equity shares of ₹ 10 each	10,00,000
12% Preference share capital	3,50,000

Company is going to produce and sell a new product. The details of the revenue and expenditure related to the product are given below:

	₹
Sale of new product	3,50,000
Less Material cost	1,00,000
Less Labour cost	1,20,000
Contribution	1,30,000
Additional Fixed cost	50,000
Operating Profit before tax	80,000
Less tax @ 35 %	28,000
Profit after tax	52,000

Calculate the value of business if capitalisation rate applicable to the company is 15%. Extraordinary items debited to current year's profit include ₹ 45,000.

Solution: Calculation of maintainable profit after tax

Profit after tax and after preference dividend	₹ 4,78,000
Add: Preference dividend	42,000
Profit after tax	5,20,000
Profit before tax (5,20,000/0.65)	8,00,000
Add: Extraordinary items debited	45,000
	8,45,000
Add: Additional profit on new product	80,000
Total Operating profit	9,25,000
Less: Tax @ 35%	3,23,750

Maintainable profits after tax	6,01,250
Capitalisation rate	15%
Value of business (Profit/0.15)	40,08,333

Value of Business from the perspective of Equity shareholders is

Value of the firm − Preference capital

40,08,333 − 3,50,000 = 36,58,333

Price Earnings Ratio: It is a ratio of Market price of equity share and Earnings per share. It is used by investment analysts, equity shareholders etc. to arrive at the market price of an equity share. For determining the Earning per share, future maintainable profit is calculated by making adjustment for expenses and incomes of exceptional nature, i.e., the ones that are not likely to appear on a regular basis, and adjustment for minority shareholders. The number of equity shares in the company is computed by taking into consideration the issue of new share and buy back of shares.

$$\text{Earnings per share} = \frac{\text{Profit available for equity shareholders}}{\text{Total number of equity shares}}$$

$$\text{Market Price of share} = \text{EPS} \times \frac{P}{E}$$

A high P/E ratio is an indication that investors are confident about the future prospects of the company and a low P/E ratio the investor's pessimistic view about the company.

P/E ratio can be found out by multiplying EPS and MPS.

Illustration 2.3: From the details given in **Illustration 2.1,** we can calculate market price per share on the basis of Price-earnings ratio.

Solution:

P/E method:

Calculation of average maintainable profits

Total profit for the last 5 years

1,80,000 + 1,60,000 + 2,10,000 + 1,80,000 + 2,00,000 = 9,30,000

$$\text{Average Profit} = \frac{9,30,000}{5} = 186,000$$

$$\text{Earnings per share} = \frac{\text{Average profit}}{\text{Number of equity shares}} = \frac{1,86,000}{60,000} = 3.10$$

P/E ratio = 8

Value per share = EPS × P/E ratio
= 3.10 × 8
= 24.80

B. Earnings Approach to Business Valuation, Cash Flow Basis:

Discounted cash flow basis of valuation is considered superior to the accounting profit method in that the latter uses the expected cash flow over a period of time. According to this method value of a firm is the present value of future cash flows expected to be generated to a firm. For the purpose future cash flow after tax is computed and the cash flows are multiplied with the present value factor. The sum total of the present values is the value of the firm. The discount rate is the rate reflecting the riskiness of the cash flows.

$$\text{Value of a firm} = \sum_{t=0}^{n} \frac{\text{CF to firm}}{(1 + K)}$$

K_0 = Overall cost of capital value of firm for all investors
K_e = Overall cost of capital for equity shareholders

Cash flow computation:

After tax operating earnings (excluding extraordinary items, income from marketable securities and non-operating investments)

Add: Depreciation

Add: Other non-cash items, say amortisation of non-tangible assets, such as patents, trademarks etc. and loss on sale of long-term assets

Less: Investment in **long-term assets**

Less: Investments in operating net **working capital**

Operating free cash flows

Add: Non-operating incomes after tax

Add: Decrease in non-operating assets like marketable securities

Free Cash Flows to Firm (FCFF)

The discount factor applicable to FCFF is overall cost of capital. Whereas in order to find out the FCFE, i.e. free cash flows to equity shareholder, interest and principal payments towards preference share capital and long-term debt are to be deducted from the FCFF, and equity capitalisation rate to be used for the purposes of calculation of present value.

Students may observe that the cash flow calculation is similar to the computation of cash flow statement.

Illustration 2.4: A company has the following capital structure:

50,00,000 equity shares of ₹ 10 each	₹ 50,00,000
12% Debentures	30,00,000

The cash flows to all investors expected over the next 5 years are

1.	30,00,000
2.	19,00,000
3.	22,00,000
4.	32,00,000
5.	41,50,000

The corporate tax applicable to the company is 40%. Compute the value of business and also value of firm from the perspective of equity shareholders. The equity capitalisation rate is 14%.

Solution:

1. **Calculation of overall cost of capital**

Capital	Amount	Cost	Proportion	WACC
Equity	50,00,000	0.14	0.625	0.0875
Debt	30,00,000	0.12 (1 − 0.40) = 0.072	0.375	0.027

WACC = 0.1145

2. **Value of Firm DCF basis**

Year	FCFF	PV factor	Total present value
1	30,00,000	0.897	26,91,000
2	19,00,000	0.805	15,29,500
3	22,00,000	0.722	15,88,400
4	32,00,000	0.648	20,73,600
5	41,50,000	0.582	24,15,300

Value of the firm   102,97,800
Less: Debt   30,00,000
Value of Equity   72,97,800

Note: Present value factor is calculated by applying the formula

$$\frac{1}{(1+k)^n}$$

For instance PV factor for year 1 = $\frac{1}{(1+0.1145)^1}$

n = Number of years, k is cost of capital.

2.2.3 Market Value based Approach to Valuation

Market value quoted in the stock market is the basis of determination of value of a business under this method. The market value of 12 months average or average of high and low values of securities during a year are used for the purpose. The average market price is multiplied with the number of securities to arrive at the value of the firm.

The limitation of the method is that the market price of securities is influenced by speculation also. Due to speculation, the market price may show a sudden change due to which the value of the firm may show an abrupt change.

2.2.4 Fair Value Method

Fair value method uses more than one method of valuation of share. It is the average of the values determined by any two or of other methods. Since it uses average value, it offsets wide variation on values.

2.2.5 Market Value Added Method (MVA)

MVA is the value added to the equity during a year. It is found out by subtracting from the market value of a firm's equity, the amount of equity investment

MVA = Market value of firm's equity – Equity capital investment

The market value of well managed companies will be high hence the MVA will also be high. On the other hand a new company or a company not managed well may even have negative MVA.

Illustration 2.5: Sunrise Company's shares are quoted in the market at ₹ 250 per share. The face value of the share is ₹ 100 each. The reserve and surplus of the company amount to ₹ 20,00,000. The Equity share capital is ₹ 1,44,000. Calculate the market value added.

Solution:

Market value of equity is 1,44,000 shares at ₹ 250 per share = 360,00,000

The equity of the company consisting of capital and reserves = 164,00,000

The MVA is ₹ 196,00,000

2.2.6 Economic Value Added Method (EVA)

It is the difference between operating profits after taxes and total cost of funds. It compares the cost of funds employed by the firm and the return on such investment. Cost of funds is the WACC or weighted average cost of capital. The accounting profit is adjusted for interest cost. The interest cost is a part of WACC.

The difference between the net operating profit and cost of funds is the real profit of the company, after considering the cost of all funds employed.

Illustration 2.6: Following information has been extracted from the Income Statement of Akshay Ltd. for the current year:

	(₹ in lakhs)
Sales	500
Less: Operating cost	300
Less: Interest cost	12
Earnings before tax	188
Less Tax (40%)	75.20
Earnings after Tax (EAT)	112.80

The firm's capital consists of ₹ 150 lakh equity funds, having 15% cost and of ₹ 100 lakh, 12% debt. Determine the EVA during the year.

Solution:

(i) Determination of net operating profit after tax

	(₹ in lakhs)
Sales	500
Less: Operating expenses	300
Less: Tax @ 40%	80
Operating profit after tax	120

(ii) Calculation of WACC

Capital	Amount ₹	Cost	Proportion	WACC
Equity share capital	150 lakh	0.15	0.6	0.09
12% Debentures	100 lakh	0.12 (1 – 0.40) = 0.072	0.4	0.0288

Weighted Average cost of capital = 0.1188

(iii) Economic Value added = Net Operating Profit after Tax – (Return expected on Capital Employed)

$$EVA = 120 \text{ lakh} - (11.88\% \text{ of total capital i.e., } 250 \text{ lakh})$$
$$= 120 - 29.70$$
$$= 90.30 \text{ lakh}$$

Practice Sums

Problem 2.1: Balance sheet of Sri Ram Ltd. as on 31st March 20.... is given below:

Liabilities	Amount ₹	Assets	Amount ₹
Equity Share Capital	20,00,000	Plant and Machinery	25,00,000
(2,00,000 shares of ₹ 10		Land and Building	15,00,000
Reserves and Surplus	18,00,000	Stock	8,00,000
12% Debentures	15,00,000	Debtors	6,00,000
Creditors	3,50,000	Cash and Bank	4,00,000
Other Liabilities	1,50,000		
	58,00,000		58,00,000

The market value of its assets are expected at

Plant and Machinery	₹ 20,00,000
Land and Building	22,00,000
Stock	7,50,000
Bad Debts	5%

You are required to compute the value of equity share on the basis of:
(a) Net Assets method, and
(b) Market value method

Solution:

Computation of Net Assets	₹	₹
Assets	**Book Value**	**Market Value**
Plant and Machinery	25,00,000	20,00,000
Land and Buildings	15,00,000	22,00,000
Stock	8,00,000	7,50,000
Debtors	6,00,000	5,70,000
Cash and Bank	4,00,000	4,00,000
Total (a)	58,00,000	59,20,000
Liabilities		
12% Debentures	15,00,000	15,00,000
Creditors	3,50,000	3,50,000
Other liabilities	1,50,000	1,50,000
Total (b)	20,00,000	20,00,000
Net Assets (a − b)	38,00,000	39,20,000
Number of equity shares	2,00,000	2,00,000
Value of share	19.00	19.60

Problem 2.2: The Balance Sheet of Chettiar & Co. is given below:

Liabilities	Amount ₹	Assets	Amount ₹
Share capital		Land and Building	9,00,000
Equity shares (of ₹ 10)	10,00,000	Plant and Machinery	8,50,000
12% Preference share	5,00,000	Equipments	1,00,000
11% Debentures	3,00,000	Stock	1,50,000
Profit and Loss Account	1,50,000	Debtors	80,000
Trade Creditors	75,000	Cash and Bank balance	20,000
Provision for Tax	80,000	Preliminary expenses	50,000
	21,05,000		21,05,000

1. The market price of the assets are:
   Land and Building   ₹ 10,00,000
   Plant and Machinery   at 10% depreciation
   Equipments   at Book value
   Stock contains shop soiled goods which are considered worthless ₹ 5,000
   Debtors require a provision of 5 % for bad and doubtful debts
   Preference dividend of one year is pending.
2. Goodwill is to be valued at 3 years purchase of the super profits based on the average of last 4 years average profit. The normal earnings of similar firms is 9%.
3. The profits of last 4 years – ₹ 1,20,000 , ₹ 1,35,000 , ₹ 80,000 , ₹ 1,10,000.

Solution:

Working for calculation of goodwill:

1. Calculation of capital employed

	₹
Land and building	10,00,000
Plant and Machinery	7,65,000
Equipment	1,00,000
Stock	1,45,000
Debtors	76,000
Cash and bank balance	20,000
Total (a)	**21,06,000**
Trade Creditors	75,000
Provision for Tax	80,000
11% Debentures	3,00,000
12% Preference share capital	5,00,000
Preference Dividend	55,000
Total (b)	**10,10,000**
Capital employed (a – b)	**10,96,000**

1. **Normal profit 9% of 1096,000 = 98640**
2. **Average profit** = (1,20,000 + 1,35,000 + 80,000 + 1,10,000)/4 = **1,11,250**
   Super profit = Average profit – normal profit
   Super profit = 1,11,250 – 98,640 = 12,610
   Goodwill = 3 × 12,610 = 37,830

Computation of Market value of share:

Market value of fixed assets and current assets	21,06,000
Add:	37,830
Total Assets	21,43,830
Less: Liabilities	10,10,000
Net Assets	**11,33,830**

Market value per share = $\dfrac{11,33,830}{1,00,000}$ = **₹ 11.3383**

Problem 2.3: Ashoka Ltd. made an after tax profit of ₹ 65,00,000 in the current financial year. The capital structure of the company consists of the following:

2,00,000 Equity shares of ₹ 10 each   ₹ 20,00,000
12% Debentures   7,50,000

Company paid tax @ 35%. Income of the company includes ₹ 60,000 profit on revaluation of assets. It made a loss of ₹ 30,000 due to fire. The capitalisation rate applicable to the company is 15%. Compute the value of business.

Solution:

Computation of future maintainable profit

Net Profit after tax	₹ 65,00,000
Profit before tax 65,00,000/0.65	₹ 100,00,000
Add: Loss due to fire	30,000
Less: Profit on revaluation	60,000
Maintainable profit before tax	99,70,000
Less: Tax @ 35%	34,89,500
Profit after tax	64,80,000

$$\text{Value of business} = \frac{\text{Profit after tax}}{\text{Capitalisation rate}}$$

$$= \frac{64,80,000}{0.15} = 43,20,3333$$

Problem 2.4: The following is the Balance Sheet of Ravi Ltd. as on 31st March .....

Liabilities	Amount ₹	Assets	Amount ₹
Share Capital		Fixed Assets:	8,00,000
1,00,000 Equity shares		Machinery	3,00,000
of ₹ 10 each	10,00,000	Factory Shed	2,00,000
Less calls in arrears	50,000	Vehicles	50,000
(₹ 2 per call)		Furniture	
Paid up capital	9,50,000	Current Assets	4,00,000
Reserves and Surplus:		Stock	7,50,000
General Reserve	4,00,000	Debtors	60,000
Profit and Loss A/c	2,30,000	Bank Balance	
Current Liabilities:		Miscellaneous Expenditure	20,000
Bank Overdraft	5,00,000	Preliminary Expenses	
Creditors	5,00,000		
	25,80,000		25,80,000

Corporate Finance   Business Valuation

The following additional information is furnished:
(i) Machinery and factory shed are worth 30% above their book value. Depreciation on appreciated value of machinery and factory shed is not to be considered for valuation of goodwill and share.
(ii) For the purpose of valuation of shares, goodwill is to be considered on the basis of 4 years purchase of super profit based on average profit (after tax) of the last 3 years. Profit of the last 3 years after tax is as follows:
For the year ended March 2004 ₹ 2,60,000
For the year ended March 2003 ₹ 3,50,000
For the year ended March 2006 ₹ 2,90,000
(iii) In the year ended 31st March 2004, new addition to Factory costing ₹ 20,000 was charged to Profit and Loss account. Depreciation charged on factory shed is 10% reducing balance method.
(iv) In a similar business, return on capital employed is 15% (after tax).
(v) Income tax @ 46%.

Find out the value of each fully paid equity share on net asset basis. Show your working to the nearest rupee.

Solution:

Value of assets:		
Machinery	(₹ 8,00,000 + 30%)	10,40,000
Factory Shed	(3,00,000 + 30%)	3,90,000
Additional Factory Shed		20,000
Less: Depreciation for 2004		2,000
Depreciation for 2005		1,800
Depreciation for 2006		1,620
Written down value		14,580
Add: Appreciation @ 30%	4,374	18,954
Vehicles		2,00,000
Furniture		50,000
Stock		4,00,000
Debtors		7,50,000
Bank		60,000
Total (a)		**29,08,954**
Less: Bank Overdraft		5,00,000
Creditors		5,00,000
Total (b)		**10,00,000**
Net Assets (a − b)		**19,08,954**

Calculation of corrected profit after tax:

Year	2004	2005	2006
Profit (after tax)	2,60,000	3,50,000	2,90,000
Add: Additional Factory Shed After Tax	10,800	–	–
Less: Depreciation on additional shed @ 10% WDV	1,080	972	875
Corrected Profit After Tax	2,68,720	3,49,028	

$$\text{Average profit} = \frac{2,69,720 + 3,49,028 + 2,89,125}{3} = 3,02,625$$

Super Profit = Average Profit – Normal Profit
= 3,02,625 – 15% of 1908,954
= 16,282

Value of Goodwill = 4 × 16282
= 65,128

Value of business and share:

Net Asset	19,08,954
Add Goodwill	65,128
Add Calls in arrears	50,000
Total Net Asset	20,24,082
Total number of shares	1,00,000
Value of fully paid share	**20.24**
Value of partly paid share (20.24 – 2.00)	**18.24**

Problem 2.5: The capital structure of a company is as follows: ₹

12% Preference shares of ₹ 10 each	5,00,000
Equity Shares of ₹ 10 each	8,00,000
Reserves and Surplus	4,00,000
10% Debentures	6,00,000
11% Term Loan	7,00,000

The average annual profit before payment of tax and interest is ₹ 6,00,000. The income tax rate is 45%.

You are required to state what valuation should be put upon the equity shares of the company if the applicable price-earnings ratio is 9. **[ICWA Final Dec. 1997]**

Solution:
Market price/Value of share = Price – Earnings ratio × Earnings per share

	₹
Calculation of EPS	
Profit before interest and tax	6,00,000
Less: Interest	
10% on Debentures	60,000
11% on Term Loan	77,000
Profit after interest	4,63,000
Less: Tax @ 45%	2,08,350
Profit after tax	2,54,650
Less: Preference Dividend	60,000
Profit for equity share holders	1,94,650
Number of Equity share	80,000
Earnings per share	2.433

$$\text{Value of equity share} = 9 \times 2.43$$
$$= 21.87$$

Problem 2.6: Accounting information of Chem Fort Ltd. is given below:

Income Statement for the year ended 31st March 2014.

	₹
Sales	1,80,00,000
EBIT	50,00,000
Less: Interest	2,00,000
EBT	48,00,000
Less Tax @ 35%	6,30,000
EAT	41,70,000

Balance Sheet as on the date

Liabilities	₹	Assets	₹
Equity Share Capital (₹ 100)	60,00,000	Freehold Land and Buildings	45,00,000
Reserves and Surplus	30,00,000	Plant and Machinery	40,00,000
10% Loan	20,00,000	Debtors	18,00,000
Creditors and other liabilities	21,00,000	Stock	23,00,000
		Cash and Bank balance	5,00,000
	1,31,00,000		1,31,00,000

Corporate Finance — Business Valuation

Additional information:

(i) Estimated future cash flows of the company are:

Year	₹
1	25,00,000
2	22,00,000
3	21,50,000
4	24,00,000
5	32,50,000

(ii) The weighted average cost of capital is 12%

(iii) Resale value of the assets are estimated at
   Freehold Land and Building   ₹ 60,00,000
   Plant and Machinery   ₹ 30,00,000
   Stock   ₹ 30,00,000
   All other assets are estimated to fetch book value.

(iv) The P/E ratio of a similar business is 7 times.

Compute the value of business and equity share based on each of the following methods of valuation:

1. Net assets method – Book value and market value
2. Price – Earnings method
3. Free Cash flow method
4. Economic value addition
5. Market value addition assuming the share is traded at ₹ 300 in the stock market.

Solution:

Net Asset Method	Book Value ₹	Market Value ₹
Freehold Land and Buildings	45,00,000	60,00,000
Plant and Machinery	40,00,000	30,00,000
Stock	23,00,000	30,00,000
Debtors	18,00,000	18,00,000
Bank and cash balance	5,00,000	5,00,000
Total (A)	1,31,00,000	131,00,000
Liabilities		

Net Asset Method	Book Value ₹	Market Value ₹
10% Loan	20,00,000	20,00,000
Creditors	21,00,000	21,00,000
Total (B)	41,00,000	41,00,000
Net Assets (A-B)	90,00,000	1,02,00,000
Value of Firm	90,00,000	1,02,00,000
Value of one share	$\frac{90,00,000}{60,000} = 150$	$\frac{1,02,00,000}{60,000} = 170$

Price Earnings method

$$\text{Value of share} = \text{Earnings per share} \times \text{P/E multiple}$$

$$= \frac{41,70,000}{60,000} \times 7$$

$$= 486.50$$

Free Cash Flow Method

Year	Free cash Flow	P.V factor @ 12%	Present Value
1	25,00,000	0.893	22,32,500
2	22,00,000	0.793	17,53,400
3	21,50,000	0.712	15,30,800
4	24,00,000	0.636	15,26,400
5	32,50,000	0.567	18,42,750

Total Present Value of cash flows = 88,85,850

Value of firm (amount for equity shareholders) = 88,85,850 – 41,00,000 = 47,85,850

Market price per share $\frac{47,85,850}{60,000} = 79.764$

Economic value added method:

$$\text{EVA} = \text{Operating profit after tax} - \text{Cost of capital employed}$$
$$= (50,00,000 - \text{tax @ 35\%}) - (12\% \text{ of } 110,00,000)$$
$$= 32,50,000 - 13,20,000$$
$$= 19,30,000$$

Market value added method:

Market value of shares – equity funds

$$= (₹ 300 \times 60,000 \text{ shares}) - (60,00,000 + 30,00,000)$$
$$= 90,00,000$$

Points to Remember

- **Valuation** is the process by which the worth of an asset, business or a security is determined. The process is undertaken by a pre-determined purpose, using an appropriate method by the experts in the field.
- **Various concepts** of value:
  1. Book Value
  2. Market Value
  3. Intrinsic Value
  4. Liquidation Value
  5. Replacement Value
  6. Salvage Value
  7. Fair Value
- **Book value** refers to the amount at which the assets and liabilities appear in the books of the company.
- **The market value** is the value or price for which a share currently trades in the marketplace, usually determined by the interaction of supply and demand for the share.
- Intrinsic Value is the rate of return expected by the equity shareholders of the company. It represents, the maximum amount purchaser would be ready to pay.
- **Liquidation value** is the price of a company's tangible assets if it goes out of business and needs to be liquidated within a limited period of time.
- **Salvage Value** is the estimated value that an asset will realise upon its sale at the end of its useful life.
- **Fair value** is the price at which property would change hands between a willing buyer and a willing seller when the former is not under any compulsion to buy and the latter is not under any compulsion to sell, both parties having reasonable knowledge of relevant facts.
- **Approaches to business valuation includes:**
  1. Asset based Valuation
  2. Earning based Valuation
  3. Market Value based Valuation
  4. Fair Value based valuation
  5. Economic value added (EVA)
  6. Market Value added (MVA)

Questions for Discussion

1. What are the objectives of business valuation?
2. Explain the following concepts of value –
   (a) Book value
   (b) Market value
   (c) Intrinsic value
   (d) Liquidation value
3. Earnings shown in the profit and loss account is to be adjusted for business valuation. Explain.
4. What are the advantages and disadvantages of Discounted Cash Flow method of business valuation?
5. Distinguish between
   (a) Market value added and Economic value added
   (b) Book value and Market value
   (c) Market value and Liquidation value

Multiple Choice Questions

1. Book value of asset includes ...
   (a) Fixed asset, current asset
   (b) Fixed asset, Current asset and intangible assets
   (c) Fixed asset, current asset, and fictitious assets
   (d) Fixed asset, current assets, intangible assets and fictitious assets
2. Under asset based method of valuation of business, liabilities include ......
   (a) Preference capital   (b) Equity capital
   (c) Equity   (d) Contingent reserve (free)
3. Market value method of business valuation is applicable to ......
   (a) Listed companies   (b) Unlisted companies
   (c) Private limited companies   (d) Public sector undertakings
4. The market price per share of a firm having equity capital of ₹ 1,00,000 consisting of shares of ₹ 10 each, profit after tax of ₹ 82,000, and P/E ratio of 8 is ......
   (a) ₹ 65.70   (b) ₹ 10.25
   (c) ₹ 65.60   (d) ₹ 1.025
5. The method of valuation suitable for an unlisted company ...
   (a) Net assets method   (b) Market value method
   (c) Market value added method   (d) None of the above

ANSWERS

| 1. (b) | 2. (a) | 3. (a) | 4. (c) | 5. (a) |

Corporate Finance — Business Valuation

Practical Problems

1. Determine the value of goodwill at 3 years purchase of the super profits based on the average of last 4 years profits from the data given below:

    Equity capital ₹ 200,00,000, Reserves and Surplus ₹ 80,00,000, normal rate of return 10%, profits made – 30,00,000, 25,00,000, 18,00,000, 31,00,000.

    [13,50,000]

2. The following is the Balance Sheet of Sun Ltd. as on 31st March 2006.

Liabilities	₹	Assets	₹
Share Capital		Machinery	6,00,000
Equity shares of ₹ 100 each	10,00,000	Factory Shed	5,00,000
Less Calls in arrears @ ₹ 20	1,00,000	Vehicles	2,00,000
Paid up capital	9,00,000	Furniture	50,000
Reserves and Surplus:		Current Assets:	
General Reserve	3,00,000	Stock	5,00,000
Profit and Loss Account	4,00,000	Debtors	6,70,000
Current Liabilities:		Bank	50,000
Bank Overdraft	3,00,000	Miscellaneous Expenditure:	
Creditors	7,00,000	Preliminary Expenses	30,000
	26,00,000		**26,00,000**

The following additional information is supplied:

(i) Machinery and factory shed are worth 30% above their book values. Depreciation on appreciated value of machinery and factory shed is not to be considered for calculation of goodwill and shares.

(ii) For the purpose of valuation of shares goodwill is to be considered on the basis of 4 years purchase of super profits based on average profit after tax of the last 3 years. Profit after tax is as follows:

    31.03.2004   ₹ 3,60,000
    31.03.2005   ₹ 4,70,000
    31.03.2006   ₹ 3,70,000

    In a similar business return on capital employed is 15% (after tax)

(iii) In the year ended 31st March, 2004, new addition to factory shed costing ₹ 20,000 was wrongly charged to Profit and Loss account. Depreciation charged on factory shed is @ 10% on reducing balance method.

Find out the value of each fully paid and partly paid share on net assets basis. Income tax is 50%. (Fully paid 247.73 and partly paid 227.73) The following particulars relate to a company:

Total Assets	₹ 18,50,000
External Liabilities	2,50,000
Share capital:	
14% Preference share of ₹ 10 each fully paid	5,00,000
40,000 Equity shares of ₹ 10 each, fully paid	4,00,000
60,000 Equity shares of ₹ 10 each, ₹ 7.50 paid	4,50,000

Calculate the value of each category of equity shares of the company based on a deemed liquidation. (12.50 and 10)

3. The following is the Balance Sheet of SB Ltd. as on March 2006.

Liabilities	₹	Assets	₹
1,00,000 Equity share of ₹ 10 each	10,00,000	Patents and Copyrights	2,00,000
		Land and Building at Cost	12,00,000
1,00,000 Equity shares of ₹ 10 each, ₹ 7.50 paid	7,50,000	Plant and Machinery at Cost	14,00,000
		Investment at Cost	1,50,000
1,00,000 equity shares of 10 each, ₹ 5 paid	5,00,00	Stock	6,00,000
		Debtors	8,00,000
Share Premium A/c	5,00,000	Bank	1,60,000
General Reserve	4,00,000	Preliminary Expenses	40,000
Profit and Loss A/c	2,00,000		
Capital Reserve	3,00,000		
Provision for Depreciation on Plant and Machinery	2,00,000		
Provision for Bad Debts	30,000		
Staff Welfare Fund	60,000		
Dividend Equalisation Fund	1,00,000		
Sundry Creditors	5,10,000		
	45,50,000		45,50,000

(i) The normal average profit after tax for the company is estimated to be ₹ 5,40,000.

(ii) The applicable capitalisation rate is 12%.

(iii) The Balance Sheet at 31st March 2006 does not contain a provision for unassessed income taxes, estimated at ₹ 75,000.

(iv) The revised value of Patent and Copyright is ₹ 1,00,000.

(v) Land and Buildings and Plant and Machinery are re-valued at ₹ 15,00,000 and ₹ 13,00,000 respectively.

(vi) Investments have a market value of ₹ 1,80,000.

(vi) Bad Debt provision should be maintained at 2% on debtors.

Calculate the value of each type of equity share by Asset Backing Method and Earning Capacity Method. (Asset method 15.96, 13.46, 10.96 earning method 20, 15, 10).

✱✱✱

Chapter 3...

Corporate Value Based Management System

Contents ...

3.1 Introduction
3.2 Shareholder's Value
3.3 Value Based Management (VBM)
    3.3.1 Meaning of VBM
    3.3.2 Features of VBM
    3.3.3 Methods of VBM
    3.3.4 Need for or Benefits of VBM
    3.3.5 Limitations of VBM
    3.3.6 Approaches to VBM
3.4 Corporate Governance
    3.4.1 Meaning and Definitions of Corporate Governance
    3.4.2 Features of Corporate Governance
    3.4.3 Difference between Corporate Governance (CG) and Corporate Management (CM)
    3.4.4 Criteria for Good Corporate Governance
    3.4.5 Models of Corporate Governance
3.5 Corporate Governance in India
3.6 Corporate Governance Clause 49
    3.6.1 Rights and Responsibilities
    3.6.2 Board of Directors
    3.6.3 Audit Committee
    3.6.4 Nomination and Remuneration Committee

3.6.5   Subsidiary Companies
3.6.6   Risk Management
3.6.7   Related Party Transactions
3.6.8   Disclosures
3.6.9   CEO/CFO Certification
3.6.10 Report on Corporate Governance
3.6.11 Compliance
- Points to Remember
- Questions for Discussion
- Multiple Choice Questions
- Project Questions

Learning Objectives...
- To understand the concept of shareholders value
- To study the concept, features, needs and benefits of value based management system
- To discuss the various approaches of value based management system
- To be able to explain the concept and criteria of good corporate governance
- To learn Clause 49 of corporate governance
- To describe the models of corporate governance

3.1 Introduction

Recent years have seen a surplus of recent management approaches for improving organisational performance: empowerment, team building, flat organisations, continuous improvement, reengineering, total quality management, kaizen, and so on. Many of them have been successful—but some of them have failed. Often the cause of failure was performance objectives that were ambiguous or not properly aligned with the ultimate goal of creating value. Value-based management (VBM) deals with this problem. It provides an unambiguous and definite metric—value—upon which an entire organisation can be built.

The thinking behind VBM is straightforward. The value of a company is determined by its discounted future cash flows. Value is created only when the returns on capital invested by companies exceeds the cost of that capital. VBM extends these concepts by focusing on how companies use them to make both major strategic and operating decisions. Properly executed, it is an approach to management that supports a company's overall objectives, analytical procedures, and management processes to focus management decision-making on the key drivers of value.

3.2 Shareholder's Value

The total economic value of an entity such as a company or business unit is the sum of the values of its equity. This value of the business is known as "corporate value" and the value of the equity part is known as "shareholder value". In short

$$\text{Corporate value} = \text{Debt} + \text{Shareholder value}$$

Shareholder value is the value enjoyed by a shareholder by acquiring shares of a company. It is the value delivered by the company to the shareholder.

Increasing the shareholder value is of prime significance for the management of a company. So the management must have the interests of shareholders in mind while making decisions. The higher the shareholder value, the better it is for the company and management.

For this to happen, management must employ efficient decision-making so as to enhance profits, thereby increasing shareholder value. On the other hand, faulty decision-making using unfair tactics might damage shareholder value.

Shareholder value is imitated in the market price of equity shares of a company. Shareholder value can also be understood as the market capitalization of the equity capital of the company at any point of time.

There has been continuous research to find out the one best management approach that will improve organisational performance. A large number of approaches have failed to achieve organisational performance due to the absence of alignment with the ultimate goal of value maximisation. According to **Timothy Koller,** "Value Based Management (VBM) tackles this problem head on. It provides a precise and unambiguous metric—value—upon which an entire organisation can be built".

3.3 Value Based Management (VBM)

3.3.1 Meaning of VBM

Value based management is the management approach that ensures that a company is run with the objective of maximising long-term and sustainable value for the shareholders. The ultimate objective, in other words is, maximisation of shareholder's return on money invested. The organisation, strategy, processes, operations, communication, evaluation, compensation and everything the company does, is aligned with this objective. In case of Japanese businesses, instead of shareholder value, it is the stakeholder's value that gets the upper hand, and in Korean counterparts, the controlling shareholder's (managers who are shareholders too) value gets the upper hand.

Under the VBM framework decision-making and all managerial processes are performed with this end in view. The interest of the Board of directors and other managers are likely to be in conflict with the interest of the shareholders. In order to align their interest with that of the shareholders of the company, the compensation system is tuned to shareholder value creation. The performance evaluation techniques adopted by the business measure the value creation by the managers.

According to **Morin and Jarrell**, "Value Based Management can be defined as a framework for targeting those business decisions that consistently add economic value to a company".

According to **Prasanna Chandra**, "It represents a synthesis of various disciplines like finance, strategy, accounting, and organisational behaviour".

VBM includes the three values:

1. **Creating Value:** The ways to increase or generate maximum future value for every decision; i.e. every decision must generate positive NPV (net present value).
2. **Managing for Value:** Governance, change management, organisational culture, communication, leadership are all aligned to value creation.
3. **Measuring value** i.e. valuation.

3.3.2 Features of VBM

1. It is an approach to management. Hence adoption of VBM affects the way managers functions—the planning, organising, decision-making, compensation, and performance evaluation.
2. The objective of shareholder value maximisation is the core to management. The company objectives, systems, strategies, processes, performance measurement and culture are all guided by this objective. In order to manage shareholder value, firms use metrics that are linked to value creation.

In some countries like Japan, it is the stakeholder value maximisation.

3. Value is said to be created when every decision which has potential to influence shareholder value, generates returns higher than the cost.
4. In order to align the interest of the managers with the objective of 'shareholder value maximisation', appropriate compensation systems are developed. The remuneration of managers is linked to value creation.

5. Value creation is measured in terms of discounted future cash flows. The net profit earned by the company is not sufficient measure of value as they do not reflect risk, do not include opportunity cost of capital and do not consider time value of money. The value of any company is equal to the present values of the future cash flows the company is expected to produce.
6. Accounting standards are modified, in the sense instead of accrual system of accounting, cash system is adopted.
7. The results are measured in terms of – Economic Value added (EVA), Cash Flow Return on Investment or Market Value Added are computed, instead of ROCE, EPS and Net Profit after tax.

3.3.3 Methods of VBM

There are several methods of VBM. The three important methods are:
1. The Free Cash Flow method
2. The Economic Value added/Market Value added method
3. The Cash Flow Return on Investment/Cash Value Added method

1. Free Cash Flow Method: The method uses weighted average cost of debt and equity i.e. WACC to discount the free cash flows. Free cash flow is the amount of cash flow available to meet the obligation of debt and equity shareholders. It is calculated as follows:

$$\text{Free Cash Flow} = \text{Profit before Interest and Tax} (1-T)$$
$$+ \text{Depreciation}$$
$$+ \text{Other non-cash items}$$
$$+ \text{Changes in Net working capital}$$
$$+ \text{Incremental investment}$$

2. Economic Value Added / Market Value Added Method (EVA/MVA)

(a) EVA: Economic Value added is the surplus left after making charge for the capital employed in the business. It can be calculated by any of the following ways:
   (i)   EVA = (ROIC – WACC) Invested Capital
   (ii) EVA = NOPAT – WACC × Invested Capital
   (iii) EVA = [PAT + INT (1 – Tax Rate) – WACC
   (iv) EVA = PAT – Cost of Equity × Equity

(b) MVA: Under the method, value is said to be created by the management when the Market Value of equity capital and debt capital is more than the Capital employed in the business.

MVA = Market value of Capital Employed – Capital employed

If the answer is positive, value is created and if the answer is negative, the value is destroyed.

Capital employed is the sum total of long-term debt and equity. Equity is the shareholder's funds. The data is collected from the Balance sheet of the company. The market value of capital employed can be found out easily if the shares and debentures of the company are listed in a stock exchange.

- Shareholder's value can be found out by deducting market value of debt from the Market value added.

Shareholder's market value added = MVA – Market value of debt

- MVA increases when NPV of cash flows increases.

Net Present Value = Present Value of Cash inflows from the project – Capital employed in the project

Or

NPV = PV Of cash inflows - capital employed

And MVA = Market value of capital employed - capital employed

That means present value of cash inflows from the project. Thus with the increase in present value of cash flows, the market value of capital increases.

2. Cash Flow Return on Investment: CFROI is the ratio of Cash Flow a company has generated to the cash invested in the company's asset in a given period. This is used by Lewis in his approach to VBM.

3.3.4 Need for or Benefits of VBM

1. VBM provides metrics on the basis of which the whole of the organisation can be built (Kotler)
2. It improves performance of the organisation as it helps in setting clear cut targets without any ambiguity. Every decision taken by the company has shareholder value maximisation as the aim.
3. Compensation of the managers is linked to performance, and hence the interest of the managers is aligned to the interest of the shareholders. Conflict of interest between board of directors and shareholder is removed. Besides mangers earn well by increasing shareholders return.
4. Shareholder value maximisation takes care of the interest of the stakeholder's (customer, suppliers, society etc.) interest as well.

3.3.5 Limitations of VBM

1. Top management support is essential for the implementation of VBM.

2. A good compensation system is required to align the interest of the people working in the company with that of shareholder value maximisation.
3. Employees need to be educated about the VBM approach. This is necessary to transform their behaviour.
4. The actual practice of VBM is important on the part of the operating managers.

3.3.6 Approaches to VBM

There are a number of approaches to VBM. These approaches define value and accordingly the indicators of performance. For some total share holder return is value for others it is economic value added and for some others it is market value added and so on. Economic value added is the most accepted approach to value based management.

1. Rapport Approach: Alfred Rapport advocates the use of Shareholder Value (SV) as a key performance indicator.

SV = Company value – Market value of debt

Company value = Net Present Value of cash flows from operations + Residual value and the marketable value of tradable securities.

Weighted average cost of capital is used to determine the present value of cash flows.

The following three important figures are to be computed:
(a) The free cash flow available to compensate debt holders and shareholders.
(b) The residual value after the planning horizon i.e. the cash flows to perpetuity.
(c) The weighted average cost of capital.

The WACC is calculated by taking the market value of capital structure. The cost of equity is determined following the Capital Asset Pricing (CAPM) model.

Shareholder value added is computed to know the change in the shareholder value over two periods.

2. Approach of Copeland/Koller/Murrin: Tom Copeland, Tim Koller and Jack Murrin advocated economic profit model. According to them

Company Value = Amount of capital invested currently + Present value of all future economic profits.

Economic profit is the difference between ROIC and WACC. In order to find out the present value, of future economic profits, WACC is used as the discounting rate.

Shareholder value (SV) is the difference between Company value and Market value of debt.

3. **Approach of Lewis:** Thomas G. Lewis advocates Total Shareholder Return (TSR) on the basis of stock price changes and dividend payments as a key performance indicator. According to him, there are three drivers that increase the Future Free Cash Flow and hence the TSR encompasses –
   (i) Increasing returns.
   (ii) Growth in activities whose returns exceed the cost of capital.
   (iii) And dividend payments, when investment in growth activities is not possible.

   The returns are measured according to CFROI. It is the ratio of cash flow a company has generated, to the cash invested in the company's asset in a given period.

   Cash value added (CVA) is the value addition, calculated as (CFROI – Cost of Capital)

   Cost of capital is calculated on the basis of broad portfolio of companies listed in the most important stock exchanges. WACC where cost of equity is calculated on the basis of CAPM is rejected by Lewis.

4. **Alcar Approach:** This approach was developed by Alcar Group Inc., a management education and software company. It is based on the discounted cash flow analysis. According to the approach company value is equal to the sum of present values of operating cash flows and present value of residual value after the planning horizon. Shareholder value is obtained by deducting the market value of debt from the company value.

   SV = PV of operating Cash Flow + PV of Residual Value – market value of Debt

   Present value of operating cash flow is the discounted operating cash flows over the period of the planning period. Present value of residual value is the present value of perpetual cash flow after the planning horizon, which is calculated by dividing the perpetual operating cash flow with the cost of capital.

Steps involved in the determination of SV
   (a) Forecast of operating annual cash flows over the planning period.
   (b) Calculate the present value of the cash flows by using WACC.
   (c) Estimate the residual value i.e., the cash flow expected after the planning horizon to perpetuity.
   (d) Find out the present value of the residual value by dividing the amount with the cost of capital.
   (e) Calculate the SV by

   $$TSV = PV \text{ of operating cash flow} + PV \text{ of residual value}$$

   (f) Calculate the Pre-strategy value, which is equal to

   $$\frac{\text{Cash flows before decision-making}}{\text{Cost of Capital}} - \text{Market value of debt}$$

(g) Find the difference between the TSV and Pre-strategy value to determine the value created.

5. Stern Stewart Approach: Stern Stewart approach is based on Economic value added. EV is the residual profit left after deducting the cost of capital employed from the operating profit after tax.

Refer to Economic value added approach to business valuation in chapter 2.

3.4 Corporate Governance

Companies are owned by shareholders but are managed by 'Board of Directors', who also owns some shares in the company. While managing the affairs, there are occasions of conflict of interest between the shareholders and the controllers of the company i.e. the board of directors. This gives rise to tensions between the two. Tensions lead to absence of communication between the parties. Lack of transparency in the functioning of the board may aggravate the situation. In practice the power to run the company is in the hands of the directors whereas the result of their actions is borne by the shareholders and others such as employees, creditors, community etc. Therefore there is a need for some system which will ensure that company is run in the best interest of its owners and stakeholders.

Corporate governance is the system that attempts to demarcate the rights and responsibilities of the stakeholders. It is like the atmosphere covering the earth. Within the framework provided by corporate governance, the objectives of the company are set and monitored. In every decision-making process the principles of corporate governance is adhered to. The interest of all the stakeholders is kept in view while setting the corporate plan and as well as during the process of execution of the plans.

3.4.1 Meaning and Definitions of Corporate Governance

Governance comes from the word **'govern'** which means to control the actions of a group for the benefit of the whole. Governance can be used in several contexts such as international governance, national governance, local governance, and corporate governance.

'Corporate' refers to the legal entity formed to transact business. Thus **'Corporate governance'** is the system by which the management of a business entity directs and controls the activities in the best interest of the stakeholders. Stakeholders are all those who have interest in an organisation such as shareholders, employees, suppliers, customers, including the members of the wider community who could be affected by environmental consequences of an organisation's activities.

Definition of Corporate Governance adopted by **Organisation for Economic Co-operation and Development (OECD)**, "Corporate Governance is the system by which business corporations are directed and controlled. The Corporate Governance structure specifies the distribution of rights and responsibilities among different participants in the corporation, such as the Board, managers, shareholders and other stakeholders and spells out the rules and procedures for making decisions in corporate affairs. By doing this, it also provides the structure through which the company objectives are set and the means of attaining those objectives and monitoring performance".

As per **Business Dictionary**, "The framework of rules and practices by which a board of directors ensures accountability, fairness, and transparency in a company's relationship with all its stakeholders (financiers, customers, management, employees, government, and the community).

In the words of **James McRitchie**, "Corporate Governance is most often viewed as both the structure and the relationships which determine corporate direction and performance. 'The Board of Directors' is typically central to corporate governance. Its relationship to the other primary participants, typically shareholders and management, is critical. Additional participants include employees, customers, suppliers, and creditors. The corporate governance framework also depends on the legal, regulatory, institutional and ethical environment of the community. Whereas the 20th century might be viewed as the age of management, the early 21st century is predicted to be more focused on governance. Both terms address control of corporations but governance has always required an examination of underlying purpose and legitimacy."

3.4.2 Features of Corporate Governance

1. Corporate governance is the framework through which corporate objectives are set and monitored. The means as well as the end is important.
2. The purpose is to balance the interest of all the stakeholders.
3. It ensures accountability, transparency and fairness on the part of the board of directors in favour of the stakeholders.
4. It governs the relationship of managers and board of directors with the shareholders and stakeholders.

3.4.3 Difference between Corporate Governance (CG) and Corporate Management (CM)

1. 'Board of Directors' is central to corporate governance. Clause 49 of the listing agreement by SEBI contains regulation on the activities and composition of Board of Directors.

    Whereas management includes all those persons in the organisation who perform managerial functions of planning, organisation, staffing, co-ordinating and controlling, it also includes the activities of the three levels of management – top level, middle level and first level managers.

2. Governance includes the policies and procedures set in place to ensure a business operates within the law and for the benefit of the stakeholders. The policies restrict or direct how people can act. For example, governance policies may include restricting the company from entering into contracts with the board members or their family members. Management includes all the actions taken by a company to lead the business to growth. Functions such as preparing budget, giving directions to the staff members, making strategic plan about marketing or product development are management functions.

3. Governance is meant to avoid conflict of interests and fraudulent activities, whereas management is more about operating business in an effective manner.

4. Governance is the system by which companies are directed and controlled whereas management is the implementation of the system.

3.4.4 Criteria for Good Corporate Governance

Following are the criteria of good corporate governance:

1. It should be law abiding. In India, Clause 49 of the listing agreement provides the principles of corporate governance. Companies must adopt those principles.

2. The best interest of all the stakeholders must be kept in view in every decision-making process.

3. It should provide transparency. Transparency means rules and regulations are followed in the decision-making process and its enforcement, that the information about the same is easily available to all those who are affected by the rules and its enforcement, and that it is available in a manner easily understandable by the concerned persons.

4. The managers and the board must be made accountable for the decisions and their implementation.

3.4.5 Models of Corporate Governance

Corporate Governance is the process by which organisations are run. There is no one model of corporate governance that is considered the best. There are many models followed in different parts of the world. Each model has its own advantage and disadvantage. Some of the important models are discussed below:

1. Continental Europe Model or German Model: This model is practiced in countries like Germany, Holland, France etc. It is a two-tiered board model. Under the model, companies of two Boards – 1. The Executive board and 2. Supervisory Board are followed.

Executive board is appointed by the supervisory board. It consists of company executives. This board is responsible for the day-to-day operations of the company.

Supervisory board on the other hand is made up of non-executive directors who are representatives of shareholders and employees of the company. It has the power to remove the member of the executive board. It determines the compensation payable to the executive board and has the power to review the major business decisions.

2. **Anglo-American Model:** This model is also known as "Anglo-Saxon" model. It is used in USA, UK, Canada, Australia, and some commonwealth countries. It is a unitary system as there is only one Board of Directors who appoints managers to manage the business. The shareholders appoint the directors. The board usually consists of executive directors and few independent directors. The Board has limited ownership stakes in the company. Both the posts of CEO of the Board and Chairman are held by the same individual, resulting in effective communication between shareholders, board and management. All important decisions are taken after consulting the shareholders.

3. **Japanese Model:** This model is also called as the 'business network model'. Usually the shareholders are banks, financial institutions, large-family shareholders, and corporates with cross-shareholding. There is a supervisory board, which is made up of board of directors and president, appointed jointly by shareholders and banks/financial institutions.

4. **Indian Model:** In India the Anglo-American Model as well as German Model is followed. Companies where promoters and their family members have control over the company, the German model is followed, and in other companies and statutory corporations Anglo-American model is found.

3.5 Corporate Governance in India

After independence India adopted mixed economy. In the beginning years of planning more importance was given to the development of public sector undertakings. But due to the failure of PSUs government started giving importance to privatisation. With the growth of the private sector, there was felt the need for good corporate governance. The first major initiative towards corporate governance was taken by the Confederation of Indian Industries (CII). It came up with voluntary code of Corporate Governance in 1948. Many companies adopted it. Since it was a voluntary code, not all listed companies adopted it. There was a need to adopt the code in order to access domestic as well as global capital at competitive rates.

In the early part of the year 2000, Securities and Exchange Board of India, took an initiative to enforce 'corporate governance' through listing agreements between companies and stock exchanges. These regulations were incorporated into Clause 49 of the listing agreement. This clause has been revised in 2002, 2003 and 2014. The main object of the revision in 2014 was to align the clause with the amended Companies Act 2013. The guideline in the clause includes such things as qualification of independent director, duties of directors, rights of shareholders, constitution of various committees including audit committee, third party transactions, and the various disclosures to be made by the company etc. Clause 49 of the listing agreement as amended in the year 2014 is given below.

3.6 Corporate Governance Clause 49

Corporate Governance norms have been reviewed by SEBI with the following objectives:
1. To align the corporate governance norms in Clause 49 of the listing agreement, with that of the provisions of the Companies Act 2013;
2. To adopt best practices of corporate governance; and
3. To make corporate governance framework more effective.

Applicability of Clause 49
(a) Provisions of the clause are applicable to all listed companies with effect from 1st October 2014.
(b) Clause 49 is applicable to other listed entities which are body corporates or are subject to regulation under other statutes like banks, financial institutes etc., and only to the extent it does not violate the provisions of the statues and guidelines or directives issued by regulatory authorities.
(c) Provision relating to 'Risk Management' is applicable to only top 100 listed companies by market capitalisation, at the end of the immediate previous financial year.
(d) Provision regarding 'related party transaction' is applicable to all prospective transactions.

Provisions under Clause 49
Clause 49 is divided into 11 parts as given below:
1. Rights and Responsibilities
2. Board of Directors
3. Audit Committee
4. Nomination and Remuneration Committee
5. Subsidiary Companies
6. Risk Management
7. Related Party Transactions
8. Disclosures

9. CEO/CFO Certification
10. Report on Corporate Governance
11. Compliance

3.6.1 Rights and Responsibilities

The company agrees to comply with the provisions of Clause 49 which shall be implemented in a manner so as to achieve the objectives of the principles as mentioned below. In case of any ambiguity, the provisions shall be interpreted and applied in alignment with the principles.

A. The Rights of Shareholders

1. The company should seek to protect and facilitate the exercise of shareholders' rights.
   (a) Shareholders should have the right to participate in, and to be sufficiently informed on, decisions concerning fundamental corporate changes.
   (b) Shareholders should have the opportunity to participate effectively and vote in general shareholder meetings.
   (c) Shareholders should be informed of the rules, including voting procedures that govern general shareholder meetings.
   (d) Shareholders should have the opportunity to ask questions to the board, to place items on the agenda of general meetings, and to propose resolutions, subject to reasonable limitations.
   (e) Effective shareholder participation in key Corporate Governance decisions, such as the nomination and election of board members, should be facilitated.
   (f) The exercise of ownership rights by all shareholders, including institutional investors, should be facilitated.
   (g) The Company should have an adequate mechanism to address the grievances of the shareholders.
   (h) Minority shareholders should be protected from abusive actions by, or in the interest of, controlling shareholders acting either directly or indirectly, and should have effective means of redress.

2. The company should provide adequate and timely information to shareholders.
   (a) Shareholders should be furnished with sufficient and timely information concerning the date, location and agenda of general meetings, as well as full and timely information regarding the issues to be discussed at the meeting.

(b) Capital structures and arrangements that enable certain shareholders to obtain a degree of control disproportionate to their equity ownership should be disclosed.

(c) All investors should be able to obtain information about the rights attached to all series and classes of shares before they purchase.

3. The company should ensure equitable treatment of all shareholders, including minority and foreign shareholders.

(a) All shareholders of the same series of a class should be treated equally.

(b) Effective shareholder participation in key Corporate Governance decisions, such as the nomination and election of board members, should be facilitated.

(c) Exercise of voting rights by foreign shareholders should be facilitated.

(d) The company should devise a framework to avoid insider trading and abusive self-dealing.

(e) Processes and procedures for general shareholder meetings should allow for equitable treatment of all shareholders.

(f) Company procedures should not make it unduly difficult or expensive to cast votes.

B. Role of Stakeholders in Corporate Governance

1. The company should recognise the rights of stakeholders and encourage co-operation between the company and the stakeholders.

(a) The rights of stakeholders that are established by law or through mutual agreements are to be respected.

(b) Stakeholders should have the opportunity to obtain effective redress for violation of their rights.

(c) Company should encourage mechanisms for employee participation.

(d) Stakeholders should have access to relevant, sufficient and reliable information on a timely and regular basis to enable them to participate in Corporate Governance process.

(e) The company should devise an effective whistle blower mechanism enabling stakeholders, including individual employees and their representative bodies, to freely communicate their concerns about illegal or unethical practices.

C. Disclosure and Transparency

1. The company should ensure timely and accurate disclosure on all material matters including the financial situation, performance, ownership, and governance of the company.

    (a) Information should be prepared and disclosed in accordance with the prescribed standards of accounting, financial and non-financial disclosure.

    (b) Channels for disseminating information should provide for equal, timely and cost efficient access to relevant information by users.

    (c) The company should maintain minutes of the meeting explicitly recording dissenting opinions, if any.

    (d) The company should implement the prescribed accounting standards in letter and spirit in the preparation of financial statements taking into consideration the interest of all stakeholders and should also ensure that the annual audit is conducted by an independent, competent and qualified auditor.

D. Responsibilities of the Board

1. Disclosure of Information

   (a) Members of the Board and key executives should be required to disclose to the board whether they, directly, indirectly or on behalf of third parties, have a material interest in any transaction or matter directly affecting the company.

   (b) The Board and top management should conduct themselves so as to meet the expectations of operational transparency to stakeholders while at the same time maintaining confidentiality of information in order to foster a culture for good decision-making.

2. Key functions of the Board

The board should fulfill certain key functions, including

   (a) Reviewing and guiding corporate strategy, major plans of action, risk policy, annual budgets and business plans; setting performance objectives; monitoring implementation and corporate performance; and overseeing major capital expenditures, acquisitions and divestments.

   (b) Monitoring the effectiveness of the company's governance practices and making changes as needed.

   (c) Selecting, compensating, monitoring and, when necessary, replacing key executives and overseeing succession planning.

(d) Aligning key executive and board remuneration with the longer term interests of the company and its shareholders.

(e) Ensuring a transparent board nomination process with the diversity of thought, experience, knowledge, perspective and gender in the Board.

(f) Monitoring and managing potential conflicts of interest of management, board members and shareholders, including misuse of corporate assets and abuse in related party transactions.

(g) Ensuring the integrity of the company's accounting and financial reporting systems, including the independent audit, and that appropriate systems of control are in place, in particular, systems for risk management, financial and operational control, and compliance with the law and relevant standards.

(h) Overseeing the process of disclosure and communications.

(i) Monitoring and reviewing Board Evaluation framework.

3. **Other Responsibilities**

(a) The Board should provide the strategic guidance to the company, ensure effective monitoring of the management and should be accountable to the company and the shareholders.

(b) The Board should set a corporate culture and the values by which executives throughout a group will behave.

(c) Board members should act on a fully informed basis, in good faith, with due diligence and care, and in the best interest of the company and the shareholders.

(d) The Board should encourage continuing directors training to ensure that the Board members are kept up to date.

(e) Where Board decisions may affect different shareholder groups differently, the Board should treat all shareholders fairly.

(f) The Board should apply high ethical standards. It should take into account the interests of stakeholders.

(g) The Board should be able to exercise objective independent judgement on corporate affairs.

(h) Boards should consider assigning a sufficient number of non-executive Board members capable of exercising independent judgement to tasks where there is a potential for conflict of interest.

(i) The Board should ensure that, while rightly encouraging positive thinking, these do not result in over-optimism that either leads to significant risks not being recognised or exposes the company to excessive risk.

(j) The Board should have the ability to 'step back' to assist executive management by challenging the assumptions underlying: strategy, strategic initiatives (such as acquisitions), risk appetite, exposures and the key areas of the company's focus.

(k) When committees of the board are established, their mandate, composition and working procedures should be well defined and disclosed by the board.

(l) Board members should be able to commit themselves effectively to their responsibilities.

(m) In order to fulfil their responsibilities, board members should have access to accurate, relevant and timely information.

(n) The Board and senior management should facilitate the Independent Directors to perform their role effectively as a Board member and also a member of a committee.

3.6.2 Board of Directors

A. Composition of Board

1. The Board of Directors of the company shall have an optimum combination of executive and non-executive directors with at least one woman director and not less than fifty percent of the Board of Directors comprising non-executive directors.

2. Where the Chairman of the Board is a non-executive director, at least one-third of the Board should comprise independent directors and in case the company does not have a regular non-executive Chairman, at least half of the Board should comprise of independent directors.

Provided that where the regular non-executive Chairman is a promoter of the company or is related to any promoter or person occupying management positions at the Board level or at one level below the Board, at least one-half of the Board of the company shall consist of independent directors.

Explanation: For the purpose of the expression "related to any promoter" referred to in sub-clause (2):

(i) If the promoter is a listed entity, its directors other than the independent directors, its employees or its nominees shall be deemed to be related to it;

(ii) If the promoter is an unlisted entity, its directors, its employees or its nominees shall be deemed to be related to it.

B. Independent Directors

1. For the purpose of the clause A, the expression 'independent director' shall mean a non-executive director, other than a nominee director of the company

    (a) who, in the opinion of the Board, is a person of integrity and possesses relevant expertise and experience;

        (i) who is or was not a promoter of the company or its holding, subsidiary or associate company;

        (ii) who is not related to promoters or directors in the company, its holding, subsidiary or associate company;

    (b) apart from receiving director's remuneration, has or had no pecuniary relationship with the company, its holding, subsidiary or associate company, or their promoters, or directors, during the two immediately preceding financial years or during the current financial year;

    (c) none of whose relatives has or had pecuniary relationship or transaction with the company, its holding, subsidiary or associate company, or their promoters, or directors, amounting to two percent. or more of its gross turnover or total income or fifty lakh rupees or such higher amount as may be prescribed, whichever is lower, during the two immediately preceding financial years or during the current financial year;

    (d) who, neither himself nor any of his relatives

        (i) holds or has held the position of a key managerial personnel or is or has been employee of the company or its holding, subsidiary or associate company in any of the three financial years immediately preceding the financial year in which he is proposed to be appointed;

        (ii) is or has been an employee or proprietor or a partner, in any of the three financial years immediately preceding the financial year in which he is proposed to be appointed, of

            (A) a firm of auditors or company secretaries in practice or cost auditors of the company or its holding, subsidiary or associate company; or

            (B) any legal or a consulting firm that has or had any transaction with the company, its holding, subsidiary or associate company amounting to ten percent or more of the gross turnover of such firm;

        (iii) holds together with his relatives two percent or more of the total voting power of the company; or

(iv) is a Chief Executive or director, by whatever name called, of any non-profit organisation that receives twenty-five percent or more of its receipts from the company, any of its promoters, directors or its holding, subsidiary or associate company or that holds two percent or more of the total voting power of the company;

(v) is a material supplier, service provider or customer or a lessor or lessee of the company;

(e) who is not less than 21 years of age.

Explanation

For the purposes of the sub-clause (1)

(i) "Associate" shall mean a company which is an "associate" as defined in Accounting Standard (AS) 23, "Accounting for Investments in Associates in Consolidated Financial Statements", issued by the Institute of Chartered Accountants of India.

(ii) "Key Managerial Personnel" shall mean "Key Managerial Personnel" as defined in section 2(51) of the Companies Act, 2013.

(iii) "Relative" shall mean "relative" as defined in section 2(77) of the Companies Act, 2013 and rules prescribed thereunder.

2. **Limit on Number of Directorships**

   (a) A person shall not serve as an independent director in more than seven listed companies.

   (b) Further, any person who is serving as a whole time director in any listed company shall serve as an independent director in not more than three listed companies.

3. **Maximum Tenure of Independent Directors**

   (a) An independent director shall hold office for a term up to five consecutive years on the Board of a company and shall be eligible for reappointment for another term of up to five consecutive years on passing of a special resolution by the company.

Provided that a person who has already served as an independent director for five years or more in a company as on October 1, 2014 shall be eligible for appointment, on completion of his present term, for one more term of up to five years only.

Provided further that an independent director, who completes his above mentioned term, shall be eligible for appointment as independent director in the company only after the expiration of three years of ceasing to be an independent director in the company.

4. **Formal Letter of Appointment to Independent Directors**

    (a) The company shall issue a formal letter of appointment to independent directors in the manner as provided in the Companies Act, 2013.

    (b) The letter of appointment along with the detailed profile of independent director shall be disclosed on the websites of the company and the Stock Exchanges not later than one working day from the date of such appointment.

5. **Performance Evaluation of Independent Directors**

    (a) The Nomination Committee shall lay down the evaluation criteria for performance evaluation of independent directors.

    (b) The company shall disclose the criteria for performance evaluation, as laid down by the Nomination Committee, in its Annual Report.

    (c) The performance evaluation of independent directors shall be done by the entire Board of Directors (excluding the director being evaluated).

    (d) On the basis of the report of performance evaluation, it shall be determined whether to extend or continue the term of appointment of the independent director.

6. **Separate Meetings of the Independent Directors**

    (a) The independent directors of the company shall hold at least one meeting in a year, without the attendance of non-independent directors and members of management. All the independent directors of the company shall strive to be present at such meetings.

    (b) The independent directors in the meeting shall, inter-alia

    (i) review the performance of non-independent directors and the Board as a whole;

    (ii) review the performance of the Chairperson of the company, taking into account the views of executive directors and non-executive directors;

    (iii) assess the quality, quantity and timeliness of flow of information between the company management and the Board that is necessary for the Board to effectively and reasonably perform their duties.

7. **Training of Independent Directors**

    (a) The company shall provide suitable training to independent directors to familiarize them with the company, their roles, rights, responsibilities in the company, nature of the industry in which the company operates, business model of the company, etc.

    (b) The details of such training imparted shall be disclosed in the Annual Report.

C. Non-executive Directors' Compensation and Disclosures

All fees/compensation, if any paid to non-executive directors, including independent directors, shall be fixed by the Board of Directors and shall require previous approval of shareholders in general meeting. The shareholders' resolution shall specify the limits for the maximum number of stock options that can be granted to non-executive directors, in any financial year and in aggregate.

Provided that the requirement of obtaining prior approval of shareholders in general meeting shall not apply to payment of sitting fees to non-executive directors, if made within the limits prescribed under the Companies Act, 2013 for payment of sitting fees without approval of the Central Government.;

Provided further that independent directors shall not be entitled to any stock option.

D. Other Provisions as to Board and Committees

1. The Board shall meet at least four times a year, with a maximum time gap of one hundred and twenty days between any two meetings. The minimum information to be made available to the Board is given in Annexure X to the Listing Agreement.
2. A director shall not be a member in more than ten committees or act as Chairman of more than five committees across all companies in which he is a director. Furthermore, every director shall inform the company about the committee positions he occupies in other companies and notify changes as and when they take place.

Explanation

1. For the purpose of considering the limit of the committees on which a director can serve, all public limited companies, whether listed or not, shall be included and all other companies including private limited companies, foreign companies and companies under Section 8 of the Companies Act, 2013 shall be excluded.
2. For the purpose of reckoning the limit under this sub-clause, Chairmanship/ membership of the Audit Committee and the Stakeholders' Relationship Committee alone shall be considered.
3. The Board shall periodically review compliance reports of all laws applicable to the company, prepared by the company as well as steps taken by the company to rectify instances of non-compliances.
4. An independent director who resigns or is removed from the Board of the Company shall be replaced by a new independent director at the earliest but not later than the immediate next Board meeting or three months from the date of such vacancy, whichever is later.

5. Provided that where the company fulfills the requirement of independent directors in its Board even without filling the vacancy created by such resignation or removal, as the case may be, the requirement of replacement by a new independent director shall not apply.

6. The Board of the company shall satisfy itself that plans are in place for orderly succession for appointments to the Board and to senior management.

E. Code of Conduct

1. The Board shall lay down a code of conduct for all Board members and senior management of the company. The code of conduct shall be posted on the website of the company.

2. All Board members and senior management personnel shall affirm compliance with the code on an annual basis. The Annual Report of the company shall contain a declaration to this effect signed by the CEO.

3. The Code of Conduct shall suitably incorporate the duties of Independent Directors as laid down in the Companies Act, 2013.

4. An independent director shall be held liable, only in respect of such acts of omission or commission by a company which had occurred with his knowledge, attributable through Board processes, and with his consent or connivance or where he had not acted diligently with respect of the provisions contained in the Listing Agreement.

Explanation: For this purpose, the term "senior management" shall mean personnel of the company who are members of its core management team excluding Board of Directors. Normally, this would comprise all members of management one level below the executive directors, including all functional heads.

F. Whistle Blower Policy

1. The company shall establish a vigil mechanism for directors and employees to report concerns about unethical behaviour, actual or suspected fraud or violation of the company's code of conduct or ethics policy.

2. This mechanism should also provide for adequate safeguards against victimisation of director(s)/employee(s) who avail of the mechanism and also provide for direct access to the Chairman of the Audit Committee in exceptional cases.

3. The details of establishment of such mechanism shall be disclosed by the company on its website and in the Board's report.

3.6.3 Audit Committee

A. Qualified and Independent Audit Committee

A qualified and independent audit committee shall be set up, giving the terms of reference subject to the following:

1. The audit committee shall have minimum three directors as members. Two-thirds of the members of audit committee shall be independent directors.
2. All members of audit committee shall be financially literate and at least one member shall have accounting or related financial management expertise.

Explanation (i): The term "financially literate" means the ability to read and understand basic financial statements i.e. balance sheet, profit and loss account, and statement of cash flows.

Explanation (ii): A member will be considered to have accounting or related financial management expertise if he or she possesses experience in finance or accounting, or requisite professional certification in accounting, or any other comparable experience or background which results in the individual's financial sophistication, including being or having been a chief executive officer, chief financial officer or other senior officer with financial oversight responsibilities.

3. The Chairman of the Audit Committee shall be an independent director;
4. The Chairman of the Audit Committee shall be present at Annual General Meeting to answer shareholder queries;
5. The Audit Committee may invite such of the executives, as it considers appropriate (and particularly the head of the finance function) to be present at the meetings of the committee, but on occasions it may also meet without the presence of any executives of the company. The finance director, head of internal audit and a representative of the statutory auditor may be present as invitees for the meetings of the audit committee;
6. The Company Secretary shall act as the secretary to the committee.

B. Meeting of Audit Committee

The Audit Committee should meet at least four times in a year and not more than four months shall elapse between two meetings. The quorum shall be either two members or one-third of the members of the audit committee whichever is greater, but there should be a minimum of two independent members present.

C. Powers of Audit Committee

The Audit Committee shall have powers, which should include the following:

1. To investigate any activity within its terms of reference.
2. To seek information from any employee.
3. To obtain outside legal or other professional advice.
4. To secure attendance of outsiders with relevant expertise, if it considers necessary.

D. Role of Audit Committee

The role of the Audit Committee shall include the following:

1. Oversight of the company's financial reporting process and the disclosure of its financial information to ensure that the financial statement is correct, sufficient and credible;
2. Recommendation for appointment, remuneration and terms of appointment of auditors of the company;
3. Approval of payment to statutory auditors for any other services rendered by the statutory auditors;
4. Reviewing, with the management, the annual financial statements and auditor's report thereon before submission to the board for approval, with particular reference to:
   (a) Matters required to be included in the Director's Responsibility Statement and to be included in the Board's report in terms of clause (c) of sub-section 3 of section 134 of the Companies Act, 2013
   (b) Changes, if any, in accounting policies and practices and reasons for the same.
   (c) Major accounting entries involving estimates based on the exercise of judgement by management.
   (d) Significant adjustments made in the financial statements arising out of audit findings.
   (e) Compliance with listing and other legal requirements relating to financial statements.
   (f) Disclosure of any related party transactions.
   (g) Qualifications in the draft audit report.
5. Reviewing, with the management, the quarterly financial statements before submission to the board for approval;

6. Reviewing, with the management, the statement of uses/application of funds raised through an issue (public issue, rights issue, preferential issue, etc.), the statement of funds utilized for purposes other than those stated in the offer document/ prospectus/notice and the report submitted by the monitoring agency monitoring the utilisation of proceeds of a public or rights issue, and making appropriate recommendations to the Board to take up steps in this matter;
7. Review and monitor the auditor's independence and performance, and effectiveness of audit process;
8. Approval or any subsequent modification of transactions of the company with related parties;
9. Scrutiny of inter-corporate loans and investments;
10. Valuation of undertakings or assets of the company, wherever it is necessary;
11. Evaluation of internal financial controls and risk management systems;
12. Reviewing, with the management, performance of statutory and internal auditors, and adequacy of the internal control systems;
13. Reviewing the adequacy of internal audit function, if any, including the structure of the internal audit department, staffing and seniority of the official heading the department, reporting structure coverage and frequency of internal audit;
14. Discussion with internal auditors of any significant findings and follow up there on;
15. Reviewing the findings of any internal investigations by the internal auditors into matters where there is suspected fraud or irregularity or a failure of internal control systems of a material nature and reporting the matter to the board;
16. Discussion with statutory auditors before the audit commences, about the nature and scope of audit as well as post-audit discussion to ascertain any area of concern;
17. Look into the reasons for substantial defaults in the payment to the depositors, debenture holders, shareholders (in case of non-payment of declared dividends) and creditors;
18. To review the functioning of the Whistle Blower mechanism;
19. Approval of appointment of CFO (i.e., the whole-time Finance Director or any other person heading the finance function or discharging that function) after assessing the qualifications, experience and background, etc. of the candidate;
20. Carrying out any other function as is mentioned in the terms of reference of the Audit Committee.

Explanation (i): The term "related party transactions" shall have the same meaning as provided in Clause 49(VII) of the Listing Agreement.

E. **Review of Information by Audit Committee**

The Audit Committee shall mandatorily review the following information:

1. Management discussion and analysis of financial condition and results of operations;
2. Statement of significant and related party transactions (as defined by the Audit Committee), submitted by management;
3. Management letters/letters of internal control weaknesses issued by the statutory auditors;
4. Internal audit reports relating to internal control weaknesses; and
5. The appointment, removal and terms of remuneration of the Chief internal auditor shall be subject to review by the Audit Committee.

3.6.4 Nomination and Remuneration Committee

A. The company shall set up a nomination and remuneration committee which shall comprise at least three directors, all of whom shall be non-executive directors and at least half shall be independent. Chairman of the committee shall be an independent director.

B. The role of the committee shall, *inter-alia*, include the following:

1. Formulation of the criteria for determining qualifications, positive attributes and independence of a director and recommend to the Board a policy, relating to the remuneration of the directors, key managerial personnel and other employees;
2. Formulation of criteria for evaluation of Independent Directors and the Board;
3. Devising a policy on Board diversity;
4. Identifying persons who are qualified to become directors and who may be appointed in senior management in accordance with the criteria laid down, and recommend to the Board their appointment and removal. The company shall disclose the remuneration policy and the evaluation criteria in its Annual Report.

C. The Chairman of the nomination and remuneration committee could be present at the Annual General Meeting, to answer the shareholders' queries. However, it would be up to the Chairman to decide who should answer the queries.

3.6.5 Subsidiary Companies

A. At least one independent director on the Board of Directors of the holding company shall be a director on the Board of Directors of a material non-listed Indian subsidiary company.

B. The Audit Committee of the listed holding company shall also review the financial statements, in particular, the investments made by the unlisted subsidiary company.

C. The minutes of the Board meetings of the unlisted subsidiary company shall be placed at the Board meeting of the listed holding company. The management should periodically bring to the attention of the Board of Directors of the listed holding company, a statement of all significant transactions and arrangements entered into by the unlisted subsidiary company.

D. The company shall formulate a policy for determining 'material' subsidiaries and such policy shall be disclosed to Stock Exchanges and in the Annual Report.

E. For the purpose of this clause, a subsidiary shall be considered as material if the investment of the company in the subsidiary exceeds twenty percent of its consolidated net worth as per the audited balance sheet of the previous financial year or if the subsidiary has generated twenty percent of the consolidated income of the company during the previous financial year.

F. No company shall dispose of shares in its material subsidiary which would reduce its shareholding (either on its own or together with other subsidiaries) to less than 50% or cease the exercise of control over the subsidiary without passing a special resolution in its General Meeting.

G. Selling, disposing and leasing of assets amounting to more than twenty percent of the assets of the material subsidiary shall require prior approval of shareholders by way of special resolution.

Explanation (i): The term "material non-listed Indian subsidiary" shall mean an unlisted subsidiary, incorporated in India, whose income or net worth (i.e. paid up capital and free reserves) exceeds 20% of the consolidated income or net worth respectively, of the listed holding company and its subsidiaries in the immediately preceding accounting year.

Explanation (ii): The term "significant transaction or arrangement" shall mean any individual transaction or arrangement that exceeds or is likely to exceed 10% of the total revenues or total expenses or total assets or total liabilities, as the case may be, of the material unlisted subsidiary for the immediately preceding accounting year.

Explanation (iii): Where a listed holding company has a listed subsidiary which is itself a holding company, the above provisions shall apply to the listed subsidiary insofar as its subsidiaries are concerned.

3.6.6 Risk Management

A. The company shall lay down procedures to inform Board members about the risk assessment and minimization procedures.

B. The Board shall be responsible for framing, implementing and monitoring the risk management plan for the company.

C. The company shall also constitute a Risk Management Committee. The Board shall define the roles and responsibilities of the Risk Management Committee and may delegate monitoring and reviewing of the risk management plan to the committee and such other functions as it may deem fit.

3.6.7 Related Party Transactions

A. A related party transaction is a transfer of resources, services or obligations between a company and a related party, regardless of whether a price is charged.

B. A 'related party' is a person or entity that is related to the company. Parties are considered to be related if one party has the ability to control the other party or exercise significant influence over the other party, directly or indirectly, in making financial and/or operating decisions and includes the following:

1. A person or a close member of that person's family is related to a company if that person:
   (a) is a related party under Section 2(76) of the Companies Act, 2013; or
   (b) has control or joint control or significant influence over the company; or
   (c) is a key management personnel of the company or of a parent of the company; or

2. An entity is related to a company if any of the following conditions applies:
   (a) The entity is a related party under Section 2(76) of the Companies Act, 2013; or
   (b) The entity and the company are members of the same group (which means that each parent, subsidiary and fellow subsidiary is related to the others); or
   (c) One entity is an associate or joint venture of the other entity (or an associate or joint venture of a member of a group of which the other entity is a member); or

(d) Both entities are joint ventures of the same third party; or

(e) One entity is a joint venture of a third entity and the other entity is an associate of the third entity; or

(f) The entity is a post-employment benefit plan for the benefit of employees of either the company or an entity related to the company. If the company is itself such a plan, the sponsoring employers are also related to the company; or

(g) The entity is controlled or jointly controlled by a person identified in (1).

(h) A person identified in (1)(b) has significant influence over the entity (or of a parent of the entity); or

Explanation: For the purpose of Clause 49(V) and Clause VII (B), the term "control" shall have the same meaning as defined in SEBI (Substantial Acquisition of Shares and Takeovers) Regulations, 2011.

C. The company shall formulate a policy on materiality of related party transactions and also on dealing with Related Party Transactions.

Provided that a transaction with a related party shall be considered material if the transaction/transactions to be entered into individually or taken together with previous transactions during a financial year, exceeds five percent of the annual turnover or twenty percent of the net worth of the company as per the last audited financial statements of the company, whichever is higher.

D. All Related Party Transactions shall require prior approval of the Audit Committee.

E. All material Related Party Transactions shall require approval of the shareholders through special resolution and the related parties shall abstain from voting on such resolutions.

3.6.8 Disclosures

A. Related Party Transactions

1. Details of all material transactions with related parties shall be disclosed quarterly along with the compliance report on corporate governance.

2. The company shall disclose the policy on dealing with Related Party Transactions on its website and also in the Annual Report.

B. Disclosure of Accounting Treatment

Where in the preparation of financial statements, a treatment different from that prescribed in an Accounting Standard has been followed, the fact shall be disclosed in the financial statements, together with the management's explanation as to why it believes such alternative treatment is more representative of the true and fair view of the underlying business transaction in the Corporate Governance Report.

C. Remuneration of Directors

1. All pecuniary relationship or transactions of the non-executive directors vis-à-vis the company shall be disclosed in the Annual Report.
2. In addition to the disclosures required under the Companies Act, 2013, the following disclosures on the remuneration of directors shall be made in the section on the corporate governance of the Annual Report:
   (a) All elements of remuneration package of individual directors summarized under major groups, such as salary, benefits, bonuses, stock options, pension etc.
   (b) Details of fixed component and performance linked incentives, along with the performance criteria.
   (c) Service contracts, notice period, severance fees.
   (d) Stock option details, if any, and whether issued at a discount as well as the period over which accrued and over which exercisable.
3. The company shall publish its criteria of making payments to non-executive directors in its annual report. Alternatively, this may be put up on the company's website and reference drawn thereto in the annual report.
4. The company shall disclose the number of shares and convertible instruments held by non-executive directors in the annual report.
5. Non-executive directors shall be required to disclose their shareholding (both theirs or held by other persons on a beneficial basis) in the listed company in which they are proposed to be appointed as directors, prior to their appointment. These details should be disclosed in the notice to the general meeting called for appointment of such director.

D. Management

1. As part of the directors' report or as an addition thereto, a Management Discussion and Analysis report should form part of the Annual Report to the shareholders. This Management Discussion and Analysis should include discussion on the following matters within the limits set by the company's competitive position:
   (a) Industry structure and developments.
   (b) Opportunities and threats.
   (c) Segment–wise or product-wise performance.
   (d) Outlook.
   (e) Risks and concerns.

(f) Internal control systems and their adequacy.

(g) Discussion on financial performance with respect to operational performance.

(h) Material developments in Human Resources/Industrial Relations front, including number of people employed.

2. Senior management shall make disclosures to the board relating to all material, financial and commercial transactions, where they have personal interest, that may have a potential conflict with the interest of the company at large (for e.g. dealing in company shares, commercial dealings with bodies, which have shareholding of management and their relatives etc.)

    Explanation: For this purpose, the term "senior management" shall mean personnel of the company who are members of its core management team excluding the Board of Directors). This would also include all members of management one level below the executive directors including all functional heads.

3. The Code of Conduct for the Board of Directors and the senior management shall be disclosed on the website of the company.

E. Shareholders

1. In case of the appointment of a new director or re-appointment of a director the shareholders must be provided with the following information:

    (a) A brief resume of the director;

    (b) Nature of his expertise in specific functional areas;

    (c) Names of companies in which the person also holds the directorship and the membership of Committees of the Board; and

    (d) Shareholding of non-executive directors as stated in Clause 49 (IV) (E) (v) above.

2. Disclosure of relationships between directors inter-se shall be made in the Annual Report, notice of appointment of a director, prospectus and letter of offer for issuances and any related filings made to the stock exchanges where the company is listed.

3. Quarterly results and presentations made by the company to analysts shall be put on the company's website, or shall be sent in such a form so as to enable the stock exchange on which the company is listed to put it on its own website.

4. A committee under the Chairmanship of a non-executive director and such other members as may be decided by the Board of the company shall be formed to specifically look into the redressal of grievances of shareholders, debenture holders and other security holders. This Committee shall be designated as 'Stakeholders

Relationship Committee' and shall consider and resolve the grievances of the security holders of the company including complaints related to transfer of shares, non-receipt of balance sheet, non-receipt of declared dividends.

5. To expedite the process of share transfers, the Board of the company shall delegate the power of share transfer to an officer or a committee or to the registrar and share transfer agents. The delegated authority shall attend to share transfer formalities at least once in a fortnight.

F. Disclosure of Resignation of Directors

1. The company shall disclose the letter of resignation along with the detailed reasons of resignation provided by the director of the company on its website not later than one working day from the date of receipt of the letter of resignation.

2. The company shall also forward a copy of the letter of resignation along with the detailed reasons of resignation to the stock exchanges not later than one working day from the date of receipt of resignation for dissemination through its website.

G. Disclosure of Formal Letter of Appointment

The letter of appointment of the independent director along with the detailed profile shall be disclosed on the websites of the company and the Stock Exchanges not later than one working day from the date of such appointment.

H. Disclosures in Annual Report

1. The details of training imparted to Independent Directors shall be disclosed in the Annual Report.

2. The details of establishment of vigil mechanism shall be disclosed by the company on its website and in the Board's report.

3. The company shall disclose the remuneration policy and the evaluation criteria in its Annual Report.

I. Proceeds from Public Issues, Rights Issue, Preferential Issues, etc.

When money is raised through an issue (public issues, rights issues, preferential issues etc.), the company shall disclose the uses/applications of funds by major category (capital expenditure, sales and marketing, working capital, etc), on a quarterly basis as a part of their quarterly declaration of financial results to the Audit Committee. Further, on an annual basis, the company shall prepare a statement of funds utilized for purposes other than those stated in the offer document/prospectus/notice and place it before the audit committee.

Such disclosure shall be made only till such time that the full money raised through the issue has been fully spent. This statement shall be certified by the statutory auditors of the company. Furthermore, where the company has appointed a monitoring agency to monitor the utilisation of proceeds of a public or rights issue, it shall place before the Audit Committee the monitoring report of such agency, upon receipt, without any delay. The audit committee shall make appropriate recommendations to the Board to take up steps in this matter.

3.6.9 CEO/CFO Certification

The CEO, i.e. the Managing Director or Manager appointed in terms of the Companies Act, 1956 and the CFO i.e. the whole-time Finance Director or any other person heading the finance function discharging that function shall certify to the Board that:

A. They have reviewed financial statements and the cash flow statement for the year and that to the best of their knowledge and belief
   1. these statements do not contain any materially untrue statement or omit any material fact or contain statements that might be misleading;
   2. these statements together present a true and fair view of the company's affairs and are in compliance with existing accounting standards, applicable laws and regulations.
B. There are, to the best of their knowledge and belief, no transactions entered into by the company during the year, which are fraudulent, illegal or violating the company's code of conduct.
C. They accept responsibility for establishing and maintaining internal controls for financial reporting and that they have evaluated the effectiveness of internal control systems of the company pertaining to financial reporting and they have disclosed to the auditors and the Audit Committee, deficiencies in the design or operation of such internal controls, if any, of which they are aware and the steps they have taken or propose to take to rectify these deficiencies.
D. They have indicated to the auditors and the Audit committee
   1. significant changes in internal control over financial reporting during the year;
   2. significant changes in accounting policies during the year and that the same have been disclosed in the notes to the financial statements; and
   3. instances of significant fraud of which they have become aware and the involvement therein, if any, of the management or an employee having a significant role in the company's internal control system over financial reporting.

3.6.10 Report on Corporate Governance

A. There shall be a separate section on Corporate Governance in the Annual Reports of company, with a detailed compliance report on Corporate Governance. Non-compliance of any mandatory requirement of this clause with reasons thereof and the extent to which the non-mandatory requirements have been adopted should be specifically highlighted. The suggested list of items to be included in this report is given in **Annexure - XII to the Listing Agreement** and list of non-mandatory requirements is given in **Annexure - XIII to the Listing Agreement.**

B. The companies shall submit a quarterly compliance report to the stock exchanges within 15 days from the close of quarter as per the format given in **Annexure - XI to the Listing Agreement**. The report shall be signed either by the Compliance Officer or the Chief Executive Officer of the company.

3.6.11 Compliance

A. The company shall obtain a certificate from either the auditors or practicing company secretaries regarding compliance of conditions of corporate governance as stipulated in this clause and annex the certificate with the directors' report, which is sent annually to all the shareholders of the company. The same certificate shall also be sent to the Stock Exchanges along with the annual report filed by the company.

B. The non-mandatory requirements given in **Annexure - XIII to the Listing Agreement** may be implemented as per the discretion of the company. However, the disclosures of the compliance with mandatory requirements and adoption (and compliance)/non-adoption of the non-mandatory requirements shall be made in the section on corporate governance of the Annual Report.

Points to Remember

- Shareholder value is the value enjoyed by a shareholder by possessing shares of a company. It is the value delivered by the company to the shareholder.
- Value Based Management can be defined as a framework for targeting those business decisions that consistently add economic value to a company.
- VBM includes the three values:
    1. **Creating Value:** The ways to increase or generate maximum future value for every decision; i.e. every decision must generate positive NPV (net present value);
    2. **Managing for Value:** Governance, change management, organisational culture, communication, leadership are all aligned to value creation;
    3. **Measuring value** i.e. valuation.

- There are several methods of VBM. The three important methods are:
  1. The Free Cash Flow method
  2. The Economic Value added/Market Value added method
  3. The Cash Flow Return on Investment/Cash Value Added method
- Free Cash Flow Method uses weighted average cost of debt and equity i.e. WACC to discount the free cash flows. Free cash flow is the amount of cash flow available to meet the obligation of debt and equity shareholders.
- Economic Value added is the surplus left after making charge for the capital employed in the business.
- Under MVA method, value is said to be created by management when the Market Value of equity capital and debt capital is more than the Capital employed in the business.
- CFROI is the ratio of Cash Flow a company has generated to the cash invested in the company's asset in a given period. This is used by Lewis in his approach to VBM.
- Corporate Governance is the system by which business corporations are directed and controlled. The Corporate Governance structure specifies the distribution of rights and responsibilities among different participants in the corporation, such as the Board, managers, shareholders and other stakeholders and spells out the rules and procedures for making decisions in corporate affairs.

Questions for Discussion

1. Define VBM. What are the benefits of implementation of value based management? What are its limitations?
2. What is VBM? What are the features of VBM?
3. Compare EVA and SVA methods of value.
4. What is Free Cash Flow method?
5. What is Corporate Governance? How is it different from Corporate Management?
6. What are the features of Corporate Governance?
7. Explain briefly the various models of Corporate Governance.
8. Who is Independent Director as per Clause 49 of the listing agreement?
9. What are the disclosures to be made as per Clause 49 of the listing agreement?
10. What is Whistle Blower's policy?
11. Who is a related party?
12. Explain the various approaches to VBM.
13. Explain the Alcar's approach to VBM in detail.
14. What is EVA? Explain the Stern Stewart approach to VBM.

15. What are the rights of shareholders as per clause 49 of the listing agreement?
16. What are the key functions of the Board of directors?
17. Explain corporate governance with regard to Audit committee?
18. What is related party transaction? What are the disclosure rules for the same?
19. What are the various disclosures to be made by companies as per Clause 49 of the listing agreement?
20. What are the responsibilities of Board as per Clause 49 of the listing agreement?

Multiple Choice Questions

1. Economic value added is calculated by the formula:
   (a) (ROIC – WACC) Invested Capital
   (b) NOPAT – Invested Capital
   (c) PAT – Cost of Equity × Equity share capital
   (d) PAT + Interest – WACC
2. Accounting information like EPS, Net Profit is not sufficient indictors of value because ......
   (a) They do not reflect risk
   (b) They do not include opportunity cost of capital
   (c) They do not consider time value of money
   (d) All the above
3. Anglo-American model of corporate governance is a ......
   (a) Two-tiered board model
   (b) Unitary board model
   (c) Consists of owner/manager board model
   (d) A combination of all
4. The executive board appointed by the supervisory board under the Continental Europe model of Corporate Governance is responsible for ......
   (a) Performance appraisal of the managers
   (b) Day to day operations
   (c) Capital budgeting decisions
   (d) All the above
5. An independent director is ......
   (a) A non-executive director
   (b) A nominee director
   (c) Was a promoter of the company
   (d) An employee of the company

6. A person cannot serve as independent director of more than ......
   (a) 5 companies
   (b) 3 companies
   (c) 7 companies
   (d) 9 companies

7. The code of conduct for all the board members and senior management of the company is to be laid down by ......
   (a) Shareholders
   (b) Board of the company
   (c) CEO of the company
   (d) Auditors of the company

8. Audit committee should meet at least
   (a) 3 times in a year
   (b) 2 times in a year
   (c) 4 times with a gap of not more than 2 months between meetings
   (d) 4 times with a gap of not more than 4 months between meetings.

ANSWERS

| 1. (a) | 2. (d) | 3. (b) | 4. (b) | 5. (a) | 6. (c) | 7. (b) | 8. (d) |

Project Questions

1. Discuss the applicability of clause 49.
2. Being the manager of ABC Limited what would be your approach to maintain the balance between creating value for the company and corporate governance norms.

Chapter 4...

Dividend Decisions

Contents ...

- 4.1 Dividend Decisions
    - 4.1.1 Introduction
    - 4.1.2 Meaning of Dividend
    - 4.1.3 Features of Dividend
    - 4.1.4 Important terms related to Dividend
    - 4.1.5 Types of Dividend
    - 4.1.6 Taxability of Dividend and Capital Gain
    - 4.1.7 Important Considerations in Dividend Policy
    - 4.1.8 Problems on Dividend Policy
- 4.2 Dividend Theories
    - 4.2.1 Dividend Relevance Theory: Walter's and Gordon's Model
    - 4.2.2 Irrelevance Theory of Dividend: Modigliani and Miller Model
- Points to Remember
- Questions for Discussion
- Multiple Choice Questions
- Practical Problems

Learning Objectives...
- To learn the meaning and characteristics of dividend
- To understand the types of dividend
- To study the important considerations in dividend policy
- To be able to explain Walter's, Gordon's and Modigliani-Miller's approach to dividend policy

4.1 Dividend Decisions

4.1.1 Introduction

Firms primarily aim to generate profits out of their business activities. The profit earned by a sole trader belongs to the trader himself who is at a liberty to decide whether to use the same for personal needs or to reinvest it in the business. Same is the case with partnership forms of businesses with a difference that decisions of profit distribution, drawing etc. are governed by the partnership deed. In other words the decisions regarding treatment of profits are taken by the partners collectively. A joint stock form of business poses a peculiar challenge in the distribution of profits due to its unique features:

(i) There is a diversion between management and ownership. The equity shareholders are the real owners of the company, whereas the management of funds, contributed by the owners, is entrusted to specialists, Board of directors. 'Whether profits are to be distributed or retained in the business', is decided by the board of directors.

(ii) The shares can be transferred by the owners of public limited companies. In case of a private limited company, shareholders may face some restrictions. If a shareholder is dissatisfied with the management of the company he can leave the company by selling off his shares. Hence board is under pressure to consider the preferences of the shareholders besides keeping in view the long term growth of the company.

4.1.2 Meaning of Dividend

The word dividend is derived from the Latin word "dividendum", meaning things to be divided. The profits divided among the shareholders of a company is called dividend. It is expressed as a certain amount on each share or as a percentage on the market price of the share.

As per the Institute of Chartered Accountants of India, "Dividend is a distribution to shareholders out of profits or reserves available for the purpose."

As per the Institute of Company Secretaries of India, "According to the generally accepted definition, dividend means the profits of a company which is not retained in the business and is distributed among the shareholders in proportion to the amount paid up on the shares held by them. Dividends are usually payable for a financial year after the final accounts are ready and the amount of distributable profits is available. Dividend for a financial year of the company (which is called the final dividend) are payable only if it is declared by the company at its annual general meeting on the recommendation of the Board of Directors."

Section 2 (22) of the Income Tax Act, 1961 defines Dividend as

(a) Any distribution by a company of accumulated profits, whether capitalised or not, if such distribution entails the release by the company to its shareholders of all or any part of the assets of the company;

(b) Any distribution to its shareholders by a company of debenture, debenture stock, or deposit certificate in any form whether with or without interest, and any distribution to its preference shareholders of shares by way of bonus to the extent to which company possesses accumulated profits, whether capitalised or not;

(c) Any distribution made to shareholders of a company on its liquidation, to the extent to which distribution is attributable to the accumulated profits of the company immediately before its liquidation, whether capitalised or not;

(d) Any distribution to its shareholders by a company on the reduction of its capital, to the extent to which the company possesses accumulated profits which arose after the end of previous year ending next before the 1st day of April 1933, whether such accumulated profits have been capitalised or not.

Companies Act

The Companies Act does not define the term dividend. It only states that dividend includes interim dividend.

According to Companies Act no dividend shall be paid by a company in respect of any share therein except to the registered shareholder of such share or to his order or to his banker and shall not be payable except cash; provided that nothing in this sub-section shall be deemed to prohibit the capitalisation of profits or reserves of a company for the purpose of issuing fully paid-up bonus shares or paying up any amount for the time being unpaid on any shares held by the members of the company; Provided further that any dividend payable in cash may be paid up by cheque or warrant or in any electronic mode to the shareholder entitled to the payment of the dividend.

In **Commissioner of Income-Tax vs. Girdha Das & Co. (Pvt. Ltd.)** it was observed that the term dividend has two meanings:

1. As applied to a company which is a going concern, it ordinarily means the portion of the profits of the company which is allocated to the holders of shares in the company;

2. In the case of winding up, it means a division of the realised assets among the creditors and contributories according to their respective rights.

4.1.3 Features of Dividend

1. It is distribution of profits of a company to its registered shareholders. Such dividend is an appropriation of profit and not an expense to the company.
2. It includes the dividend paid at the time of liquidation of a company to the creditors and contributories out of the realised amount of assets.
3. Dividend cannot be paid out of capital of a company.
4. Dividend can be an interim dividend or a final dividend. Final dividend is paid at the end of a financial year, whereas interim dividend is paid in between two Balance Sheet dates.
5. The rate of Dividend on equity share is recommended by the directors and declared by the company. It is stated as a fixed amount per share.
6. Dividend can be paid in the form of cash or share or any asset of the company. The latter is called issue of bonus share.
7. There exists an inverse relationship between dividend to shareholders and retained earnings. Usually stable companies issue dividends. Their share prices may not move, hence the dividend is paid to compensate the shareholder who is not earning out of capital appreciation. High growth companies do not distribute their entire profit as dividend. Rather a major amount is retained for expansion purpose as it is a low cost source of finance for the firm.
8. In India dividend on equity shares received by a shareholder is exempt from tax in the hands of the shareholder. Company is required to pay Dividend Distribution Tax (DDT).

4.1.4 Important terms related to Dividend

Some terms that are related to dividend are explained here:

1. Dividend per Share (DPS): With respect to equity shareholders it means the dividend payable per equity share. It is in the form of a certain amount. Dividends are declared normally as dividend per share, besides being expressed in the form of dividend yield. It is calculated by the following formula:

$$\text{Dividend per share} = \frac{\text{Dividend paid to equity shareholders}}{\text{Number of equity shares}}$$

2. Dividend Pay-out Ratio: It is the ratio between the 'dividend per share' (DPS) and 'earning per share' (EPS) of a company. It indicates the part of earning of the company paid by way of dividend. 100% payout means company has distributed all its earnings i.e., net profits to the shareholders. On the other hand 0 payout means the company has retained all its profits for future use and has not distributed any amount to the shareholders. A growth oriented company which has lot of investment opportunity may not pay dividend to shareholders as it would keep the profits for reinvestment in the business.

Formula for calculating dividend payout ratio is

$$\text{Dividend payout} = \frac{\text{Dividend per share}}{\text{Earning per share}} \times 100$$

3. **Dividend Yield:** It is the ratio of dividend per share and market price of the share. Investors are more interested to know as to how much their investment is earning for them.

$$\text{Dividend yield} = \frac{\text{DPS}}{\text{Market price per share}}$$

4. **Dividend Cover:** It shows the number of times the dividend to ordinary shareholders of a company is covered by the profit of the company after tax. It is calculated by dividing the net earnings of the company by the dividend amount.

$$\text{Dividend cover} = \frac{\text{Net profit after tax and after preference dividend}}{\text{Dividend to equity shareholders}}$$

5. **Dividend Warrant:** It is an instrument issued by a company to its registered shareholders stating the amount of dividend payable to the concerned shareholder asking the banker of the company to pay the specified amount to the shareholder or to his order. It is in two parts:

   (a) The notice of dividend to the shareholder.
   (b) Details of the meeting which declared the dividend, the rate of dividend, the period to which the dividend is declared, the gross and the net amount of dividend payable to the shareholder named therein or to his order.

6. **Dividend Policy:** The policy of the management of a company regarding the division of its net earning between 'dividend to shareholders' and 'retained earning' is called the dividend policy. Growth companies do not pay much dividend as they need the profits for further investment into its business. Shareholders, in such cases get the benefit of appreciation in the price of the shares held by them. A stable company may pay high dividend out of the profits, to compensate the shareholders for stagnancy in the market price of the share of the company. A normal company may retain a part for future investment and utilise the remaining part for payment of dividend. There are a number of factors that influence the dividend policy of a company. These are discussed later in this chapter.

7. **Dividend Theory:** Dividend theory analyses the relationship between 'dividend policy of a firm' and 'value of the firm'. It examines as to how the dividend decision of the firm affects the market price of the share and hence the 'value of the firm'. There are two sets of theories that are discussed in this chapter–

(a) The dividend relevance theories; and
(b) Dividend irrelevance theory.

These theories explain the impact of dividend on the share price under certain assumptions and prove their point by way of mathematical formulae.

4.1.5 Types of Dividend

The chart below shows the various types of dividend:

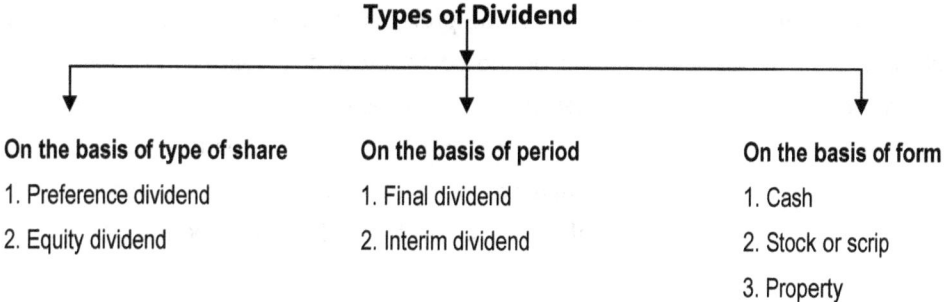

I. On the basis of types of shares there can be two types of dividend which corporates pay. The dividend on preference share is called **'preference dividend'**. This dividend is fixed in advance and hence does not change with the increase in the earnings of the company. If company declares dividend the preference share holders get their dividend at a certain percentage of the face value of the share. The dividend paid to the equity shareholders of a company is called **equity dividend**. The rate of equity dividend is not predetermined. It may change depending on the profits of the company. It is expressed as a certain amount per share or as a percentage of the market price of the share. It is declared by the company in its annual general meeting. The amount of dividend is recommended by the board of directors of the company. The company cannot declare a higher rate of dividend than that is recommended by the board. Directors may declare dividend after announcing their quarterly results as well.

II. On the basis of periodicity of dividend there can be (a) Final dividend, (b) Interim dividend.

Final dividend is declared by the company in its annual general meeting, as per the recommendation of the directors of the company. The members may reduce the dividend but cannot increase it beyond the amount so recommended by the board. Final dividend is payable out of the annual net earnings of the company at the end of the financial year. Interim dividend on the other hand is declared by the board of directors after the interim financial reports like quarterly performance report.

III. On the basis of the form in which dividend is paid by a company there can be cash dividend, issue of bonus shares, or property dividend. **Cash dividend** is the most common form of dividend. A company which has made profits and has cash balance can declare cash dividend. Payment of cash dividend includes payment in the form of cheque or dividend warrant. This kind of dividend reduces the profits of the company on one hand and cash and bank balance on the other. Companies facing liquidity crunch do not pay cash dividend.

Some companies at developmental stage prefer **stock dividend**. This kind of dividend results in ploughing back the profits of the company and increases the total number of shares in the hands of its shareholder. If market prices of shares increase the shareholders gain immensely in terms of wealth. This type of dividend is called bonus shares. Bonus can be issued to convert the partly paid up shares of the shareholder into fully paid shares. There are regulations applicable to the issue of bonus shares by SEBI and Companies Act, which must be abided by the company.

There is the third form of dividend which is not very popular i.e., payment of dividend in the form of **properties** held by a company. A company may distribute the unused properties to its shareholders in the form of dividend.

4.1.6 Taxability of Dividend and Capital Gain

Shareholders of a company can earn two kinds of income out of their investment in the shares of a company – dividend and capital gain.

1. **Dividend:** It is the distribution of net earnings of the company to the registered shareholders. As per the Indian Income Tax Act, dividend income from a Domestic Company is not taxable in the hands of the recipients. Thus for the shareholders, it is tax free income. But company has to pay Dividend Distribution tax (DDT) @ of 12.5 % on the dividend distributed by it.

2. **Capital Gain:** Shareholders of listed companies can sell off their share in the stock market and make profit on the sale. Such profit is termed as capital gain. Capital gain is called Long-Term Capital gain (LTCG) if concerned shares were held for a period of more than 12 months before such sale. LTCG on sale of share is not taxable as the government wants to encourage long-term investment in companies. On the other hand if shares were held for a period of 12 months or less before sale, then the gain made on such sale is termed as Short-Term Capital Gain (STCG) and is taxable @ 15% if Securities Transaction Tax has been paid.

4.1.7 Important Considerations in Dividend Policy

Dividend policy refers to the policy of a firm with regard to the apportionment of net earnings of the company into 'dividend to shareholders' and 'retained earnings'. The decision regarding dividend policy is a tough one. It has an impact on the future earnings of the company as well as on the market price of its shares. Hence it has a strong influence on the 'wealth maximisation' goal of the firm. A company must carefully consider various factors before deciding about its dividend policy. The important considerations can be grouped as under:

1. Economy
2. Legal
3. Industry
4. Stability of dividend
5. Owner
6. Internal considerations

1. Economy: Firms cannot detach themselves from the economy in which they are operating. The level of business activity and the net earnings of a firm depend on the general economic and business conditions prevalent in the economy. The economy related factors are to be considered while deciding about the dividend payout. In developing economies there is a great demand for resources, including financial resources. The firms in such economies may have to adopt lower dividend payout and higher retention ratios to finance their future ventures. In developed economies companies may adopt liberal dividend payout.

Business cycle of the economy influences the dividend decisions. During the boom period, although earnings of the firm are high, it may adopt a low dividend payout policy. On the other hand during recession a high rate of dividend may be paid out due to fear of insolvency.

Capital markets are important pillars of an economy. Larger the number of investors in the capital market easier it would be for the organisations to raise funds. In India the government is giving lot of importance to increase the number of retail investors by adopting investor education programmes, tax concessions, regulations to protect the principal of the investors etc. If the capital market is well regulated, the investors would feel confident to invest in the market. On the other hand if regulatory authorities are inefficient, the investors would lose confidence in the capital market instrument, thereby making it tough for the firms to raise funds from the market. In such a case firms will depend on internally generated funds and pay low amounts of dividend to the shareholders.

Inflation is another important consideration. Due to rising prices, firms may not be able to replace their fixed assets by using the depreciation provision alone. Additional funds would be required to purchase another asset. During inflation, therefore companies would adopt a low dividend policy or no dividend if the asset has to be replaced in the near future.

2. **Legal:** There are laws that intend to protect the investors and the shareholders of a company. The dividend policy of a company must be within the provisions of the law. As per *Companies Act* no dividend can be paid out of the capital of the company, only revenue profits earned can be distributed as dividend. According to the provisions of the said act, a company must transfer prescribed percentage of the net profit, not exceeding 10%, to the reserves of the company. The company can transfer more than the prescribed percentage. A company cannot declare any dividend if it fails to redeem the redeemable preference shares due for redemption.

Besides, payment of dividend in the form of bonus share is regulated by *Securities and Exchange Board of India*. It has issued guidelines to be followed by companies while making bonus issue.

Income Tax Act provides tax on the incomes of the shareholders as well as the company. At present companies are required to pay Dividend Distribution Tax on the amount of dividend distributed by them. The dividend income received from a domestic company is not taxable in the hands of the shareholders. The gain made of sale of shares is taxable as per the rule under capital gain of the tax act. Taxation is one of the considerations that affect the preference of the shareholders between dividend and capital gain.

3. **Industry:** Industries that have stable earnings like public utilities and basic industries like steel industries are in a position to declare stable dividend than firms in the other industries. Another point to be considered is the dividend paid by other firms in the industry.

4. **Stability of Dividend:** Firms need to have stability in dividend policy as investors prefer stable dividend. It implies that a certain amount of dividend is paid regularly, without much variability in dividend stream. A stable dividend policy demands commitment on the part of the management. Stability of dividend may take any of the following forms:

(i) **Predetermined Amount of Dividend per Share:** According to this form, companies decide the fixed amount of dividend they would pay year after year. Net earnings of the company might increase or decrease but the dividend per share would not change. This implies the firm must keep reserves to make up for the deficiency in the amount of dividend in the years when the net earnings are low.

The DPS is increased when the net earnings of the company increases and the increase is expected to be maintained.

(ii) **Certain Percentage of Net Earnings or Certain Payout Ratio:** Under this form of policy companies decide the percentage of EPS company is ready to pay as dividend. For example company might decide to pay 50% of the net earnings. The balance of the earning would be retained. The dividend per share would increase or decrease with the change in the net profits of the company. The best part of this method is in times when company is making less profit automatically the dividend is also reduced. Company won't pay any dividend if it has not earned any profit.

(iii) **Constant Dividend per Share with Extra Dividend in Times of Prosperity:** This kind of stability may be preferred by the shareholders as under the method a certain minimum amount of dividend per share is assured with an extra dividend in times of prosperity. As soon as normal condition is restored, company would pay the normal dividend.

(iv) **Fixed Amount of Dividend with Consistent Increase:** Shareholders get a fixed amount per share as dividend. The amount is increased consistently with the growth of the earnings of the company. This can be adopted when company is expected to grow consistently.

(v) **Dividend as a Percentage on the Market Price of Share:** Shareholders like to know the return on market price of their share. Hence this method requires the setting up of the target rate based on the rate of other competing firms in the industry or a rate which is average in the Industry. Under this method DPS would change with the change in market price of the share. In efficient capital markets, market price reflects the value of the business. But the market price may not reflect the real worth of the business due to inefficiencies in the market.

5. **Owner**

(i) **Types of Owners:** The owners of a company may consist of institutional investors and retail investors. The preferences of the two categories of shareholders may be different and must be incorporated in the dividend policy.

(ii) **Dilution of Control:** If the owners are averse to dilution of control, then the company will not be able to raise funds by issuing equity shares. It will have to rely on retained earnings or borrowings. In such a case companies would pay low amounts of dividends and retain major part of their earnings.

(iii) **Widely Scattered Shareholders:** In companies where the distribution of shares is among a small number of owners, it is possible for the company to know their preferences and accordingly decide about dividend payment. Further it is possible to convince them as to how the payment or non-payment of dividend would be in their interest in the long run. In case of large number of shareholders it is not possible. In such cases a standard method of dividend payout may be adopted.

6. **Internal Considerations**
(i) **Company's Investment Opportunities:** Firms having investment opportunities would like to retain their net earnings for further investment, as the other sources of finances are costlier and involve lot of legal formalities when compared to the internal source of finance.
(ii) **Age:** A company which is not still new would retain its earning rather than distributing it to the shareholders. On the other hand, an established company which has less scope for growth would be liberal with its dividend policy.
(iii) **Need for Finance:** A company which is in need of funds in the near future would have higher retention and lower payout ratio.
(iv) **Other Sources:** A company that does not have easy access to other sources of finance like loan, issue of bonds etc. would rely on internally generated funds and hence would pay low dividends even when it makes large profits.
(v) **Cash Position:** Cash dividend requires large amount of liquid assets in the form of cash and bank balances. Many profit making companies face the problems of cash crunch partly due to the funds being tied up in long-term commitments and partly due to aggressive credit sales and other varied reasons. Such companies will be compelled to retain net earnings.
(vi) **Earning Capacity:** Dividend is paid out of the net earnings of a company. If the earnings are low the company cannot pay high dividends. The earning capacity of a firm directly affects the dividend payout. Besides, creditors may demand low payout, so that they may not have to face defaults in interest payment and debt repayment.
(vii) **Agreements or Contracts:** Sometimes as per the agreement with the creditors or lenders, the dividend payout ratios may be kept low by companies.

4.1.8 Problems on Dividend Policy

Problem 4.1: Arogya Ltd. follows 'Constant dividend per share' policy. Assuming that it is required to transfer a minimum of 10% of its earnings to reserve, calculate the amount of dividend payable to the shareholders and the amount of retained earnings that would result at the end of the 5th year. The expected net earnings of the company are given as follows.

1st year ₹ 30,00,000
2nd year ₹ 10,00,000
3rd year ₹ 6,00,000
4th year ₹ 15,00,000
5th year ₹ 20,00,000

The number of shares outstanding is ₹ 10,00,000 @ ₹ 10 per share.

Solution: Amount available for dividend is 90% of the net earnings as 10% is transferred to the Reserve.

Year	Net earnings	Reserve	Dividend amount	Dividend per share (D/shares)
1	30,00,000	3,00,000	27,00,000	27
2	10,00,000	1,00,000	9,00,000	9
3	6,00,000	60,000	5,40,000	5.40
4	15,00,000	1,50,000	13,50,000	13.50
5	20,00,000	2,00,000	18,00,000	18

(a) The minimum amount of dividend is ₹ 5.40 per share. Since the company wants to follow constant dividend per share it can pay ₹ 5.40 per share as dividend.

(b) The amount of retained earnings at the end of the 5th year would be equal to the total amount of net earnings in the 5 years minus the dividend paid in the 5 years.
₹ 81,00,000 – 5 (1,00,000 shares @ ₹ 5.40) = 54,00,000

Problem 4.2: Capital structure of BEC Industries Ltd. is given below:

2,50,000 equity shares of ₹ 10 each	₹ 25,00,000
10% 50,000 preference shares of ₹ 10 each	₹ 5,00,000
General reserve	₹ 3,00,000
Net profits after tax for the current year	₹ 20,00,000
Cash and bank balance	₹ 12,00,000

The company is required to transfer 10% of its net earnings after tax to the reserve. The company wants to pay dividend to the shareholders out of the current earnings only. It needs ₹ 80,000 cash for its immediate working capital needs.

(i) Calculate the maximum dividend payable per share out of the current year's earnings.

(ii) If the company does not want to take overdraft facility, how much cash dividend can be paid per share?

Solution:

Net profit available for distribution as dividend to equity shareholders is –

Net profit after tax – 10% transfer to reserve – Preference dividend

20,00,000 – 2,00,000 – 50,000(10% of 5,00,000)

= 17,50,000

(i) DPS = $\dfrac{17,50,000}{2,50,000}$ = ₹ 7 per share

(ii) Total cash balance available for dividend = Cash balance – Working capital needs – Preference dividend

₹ 12,00,000 – 80,000 – 50,000 = 10,70,000

DPS when company does not borrow for dividend payment = $\dfrac{10,70,000}{2,50,000}$ = ₹ 4.28

Problem 4.3: Rayagada Paper Ltd. expects the following amounts of earnings for the next 6 years of its functioning:

Years	Earning per share	Market Price
1	20	90
2	25	91
3	15	88
4	8	80
5	22	90
6	23	94

Calculate the dividend payable by the company under each of the following methods and give your opinion about the best dividend policy.

(i) Company pays ₹ 12 per share as dividend.
(ii) Company's D/P ratio is 60%.
(iii) Company decides to pay ₹ 12 per share as dividend for 1st and 2nd year and to increase the amount by 10% in the 3rd year and 4th year and again increase it by 10% in the 5th and 6th year.
(iv) The target rate of dividend is 15% of the market price.

Solution:

Years	Earning per share	(i) DPS	(ii) DPS	(iii) DPS	(iv) DPS
1	20	12	12	12	13.50
2	25	12	15	12	13.65
3	15	12	9	13.20	13.20
4	8	12	4.80	13.20	12
5	22	12	13.20	14.52	13.50
6	23	12	13.80	14.52	14.10

Investors prefer a constant dividend policy with consistent growth as dividend. It gives them income regularly with predictability in the amount of dividend. In the case of the above example, the third policy of paying ₹ 12 as dividend and increasing the amount by 10% every two years might be preferred by the investors. The dividend yield method also is giving a somewhat consistent dividend due to less fluctuation in the market price of the share. But it may not be true for all companies at all times.

4.2 Dividend Theories

Dividend theories study the impact of dividend policy of a firm on the market price of the share and consequently on the value of a firm. There are contradictory theories advocated by experts in the subject. According to one school of thought, the dividend policy affects the market price of the share of the company. The investment policy and dividend policy are interdependent. The opposite view is held by other school of thought which advocates that dividend policies do not have any influence over the value of the firm. The investment decisions are independent of the dividend decisions of the firm. The value of the firm depends on the earning capacity of the firm and its assets, not on its dividend policy.

4.2.1 Dividend Relevance Theory: Walter's and Gordon's Model

Two important dividend relevance theories are:
1. Walter's Model; and
2. Gordon's model

(A) Walter's Model

According to this model, investment decisions and dividend decisions of a firm are interlinked. The dividend decision of the firm influences the market price and the value of the firm when the rate of earning of the firm and the expected rate if earning of the shareholders are different. It may be noted that the expectation of the shareholder is built on the basis of the external investment opportunities available to them. It is also called as the opportunity cost for the company. If the two rates are equal which is rarely possible, the dividend policy won't affect the value of the company.

The theory is based on the following assumptions:

(i) Company depends on internal financing alone; it doesn't have access to other external sources of financing such as bank loan, issue of debentures and bonds etc.

(ii) The rate of return on the investment of the firm and the cost of capital i.e., the expected rate of return of the shareholder is constant.

(iii) The net profits of the company are either distributed as dividend or re-invested in the company.

(iv) The firm has a long life.

According to this model, firms should use their net earnings for re-investment in the business itself, if suitable investment opportunities are available i.e., the investment which will generate a return higher than that is expected by the shareholders. The rate of return earned by the firm on its investment within the firm is denoted as 'r'.

Investment opportunities are available to the shareholders as well. They can invest the dividend income in avenues outside the firm and earn further income. The expected rate of return from outside investment is the opportunity cost of the company. It is expressed as 'K_e' or 'k'. If 'k' is higher than 'r' the company should use its net earnings in paying dividend. By paying dividend, in such situations, the company allows the shareholders to invest their dividend income outside the firm and earn higher return.

Thus investment decision of a firm is related to its dividend decision and the key factors are the two rates - the internal rate of return 'r' of the company and the cost of capital 'k'.

(a) When (r > k), a decrease in payout ratio will increase the market price of the share of the company and the value of the business. The optimum payout ratio is 0%. In other words the firm should retain the earnings to increase the value of the business.

(b) When (r < k), an increase in the payout ratio would lead to a rise in the market price of the share of the company and consequently the value of the business. The optimum dividend policy would be to distribute all the earnings to the shareholders as dividend. This would increase the market price of the share of the company as the policy allows the shareholders to invest in better avenues outside the business.

(c) When (r = k), dividend policy will be irrelevant. The price of the share in the market and the value of the business would not depend on the dividend policy of the firm. The shareholders would be indifferent towards the payout policy of the firm.

Corporate Finance   Dividend Decisions

Walter's mathematical formula:

$$P = \frac{D}{k} + \frac{r\frac{(E-D)}{k}}{k}$$

or

$$P = \frac{D + \frac{r}{k}(E-D)}{k}$$

P = Market price of the share
D = Dividend per share
E = Earnings per share
r = Internal rate of return
k = Cost of capital or capitalisation rate
(E − D) = Retained earnings per share

According to the mathematical formula, price per share is a sum of two components –

(i) $\frac{D}{k}$: It is the present value of an infinite stream of dividends.

(ii) $\frac{\frac{r}{k}(E-D)}{k}$: It is the present value of an infinite stream of returns from retained earnings.

Problem 4.4: Determine the price of the share of a company from the following details, assuming Walter's assumptions hold.

Cost of capital is 12%. Company is paying ₹ 3 per share as dividend out of its total earnings of ₹ 50,00,000. The number of shares outstanding is 10,00,000. Assuming the company can generate a return of 15% on its investment, what will be the share price? Calculate the price when the return on company's investment is (i) 12%, as well as when it is 10%.

What will happen to the share price if the company decides to have
1. 100% payout, and
2. 100% retention i.e. 0% dividend pay put

Solution:

Given:

Cost of capital 'k' = 12%

Return on investment 'r' = 15% or 12% or 10%.

Dividend per share 'D' = 3

Earnings per share 'E' = $\dfrac{\text{Earnings}}{\text{Number of shares}} = \dfrac{50,00,000}{10,00,000} = 5$

Price of share, when r > k i.e. r = .15 /.12 /.10 and k = 0.12

The formula as per Walter's Model is $P = \dfrac{d + \dfrac{r}{k}(E - D)}{k}$

By substituting the values in the given equation we get

(i) When r > k

$$P = \dfrac{3 + \dfrac{0.15}{0.12}(5 - 3)}{0.12} = 45.833$$

(ii) When r = k, r = 0.12 we get

$$P = \dfrac{3 + \dfrac{0.12}{0.12}(5 - 3)}{0.12} = 41.667$$

(iii) When r < k, r = 0.10 we get

$$P = \dfrac{3 + \dfrac{0.10}{0.12}(5 - 3)}{0.12} = 38.889$$

1. **If the company adopts 100% payout ratio the market price of the share will be**

    (i) When r > k i.e. r is 15%

    $$P = \dfrac{5 + \dfrac{0.15}{0.12}(5 - 5)}{0.12} = 41.667$$

    (ii) When r = k i.e. r is 12%

    $$P = \dfrac{5 + \dfrac{0.12}{0.12}(5 - 5)}{0.12} = 41.667$$

    (iii) When r < k, r = 0.10 we get

    $$P = \dfrac{5 + \dfrac{0.10}{0.12}(5 - 3)}{0.12} = 41.667$$

2. **If the company adopts 100% retention i.e. decides not to pay dividend, then share prices will be –**

   (i) When r > k i.e., r is 15%

   $$P = \frac{0 + \frac{0.15}{0.12}(5 - 0)}{0.12} = 52.00$$

   (ii) When r = k i.e., r is 12%

   $$P = \frac{0 + \frac{0.12}{0.12}(5 - 0)}{0.12} = 41.667$$

   (iii) When r < k, r = 0.10, we get

   $$P = \frac{0 + \frac{0.10}{0.12}(5 - 0)}{0.12} = 34.72$$

Evaluation:

(a) When r > k the highest market price is achieved by resorting to 100% retention of 0% dividend payout. As per the model, when internal rate of the company is higher than the opportunity cost of the shareholders, the company should retain its earning in order to raise the market value of share and value of business.

(b) When r = k under all circumstances i.e. when it pays ₹ 3 as dividend, ₹ 5 as dividend and 0 as dividend, the market price of the share remains at ₹ 41.667. It means dividend policy of the company does not exert any influence on the market price of the shares of the company.

(c) When r < k, the market price is highest when company adopts 100% payout.

(B) Gordon's Model

Gordon's theory of dividend policy favours the dividend relevance theory. It is based on the assumption that investors are risk averse, hence prefer current dividend to future dividend and capital appreciation. Future is uncertain both with regard to payment of dividend and timing of the payment. Hence as the retention ratio increases the investors discount the future earnings at a higher rate. They place lower value on the future earnings of the firm. The theory is based on the old saying – "a bird in the hand is worth two in the bush". What is available now is better than what might be available in the future even if the benefit happens to be more than that of the current benefit.

Corporate Finance   Dividend Decisions

The model is based on the following assumptions:
(i) Retained earnings are the only source of finance for the company.
(ii) The rate of return of the firm and the cost of capital are constant.
(iii) The growth rate of the firm remains constant and is lower than the cost of capital. The growth rate is the product of the retention ratio and the rate of return.
(iv) The firm has a perpetual life.
(v) There are no taxes.

The concept of growth rate is not discussed in the Walter's model. The assumptions of the two models are same. But the mathematical formula of Gordon's model is based on the dividend capitalisation model of business valuation. The formula for the determination of market price of the shares of the company is

$$P = \frac{E(1-b)}{k_e - br}$$

P = Market price of the share of the firm
E = Earnings per share
b = Retention ratio
(1 − b) = Dividend payout ratio
K_e = Cost of equity capital
br = Growth rate

Problem 4.5: From the following particulars of a company, compute the market price of its shares on the basis of Gordon's model and comment on the results.

Earnings per share = ₹ 10

Retention ratio is 75%

Cost of equity is 12% and internal rate of return of the company is 14%

Also calculate the price of share if the rate of return is 10% and when the rate is 12%.

Solution:

Given:
$$E = 10$$
$$r = 0.14/0.10$$
$$k_e = 0.12$$
$$b = 0.75$$
$$(1 - b) = 0.25$$
$$br = (0.75 \times 0.14)$$
$$= 0.105 \text{ or } (0.75 \times 0.10)$$
$$= 0.075 \text{ or } (0.75 \times 0.12)$$
$$= 0.09$$

Substituting the figures in the formula, $P = \dfrac{E(1-b)}{k-br}$

$$= \dfrac{10(0.25)}{0.12 - 0.105} = 166.67 \ [r > k]$$

When r is 10% $\quad P = \dfrac{10(0.25)}{0.12 - 0.75} = 55.556 \ [r < k]$

When r is 12% $\quad P = \dfrac{10(0.25)}{0.12 - 0.09} = 83.33 \ [r = k]$

It may be noted here that when 'r' is more than 'k', the retention of 75% of the net earnings is resulting in higher share price than when 'r' is less than 'k'. In the second situation the company can increase the market price by paying higher amounts of dividend. Say the retention rate of 75% is converted into 25%. The market price of share will be

When r = 14% $\quad P = \dfrac{10(0.75)}{0.12 - (0.25 \times 0.14)} = \dfrac{7.5}{0.085} = 88.23 \ [r > k]$

When r = 10% $\quad P = \dfrac{10(0.75)}{0.12 - (0.25 \times 0.10)} = \dfrac{7.5}{0.095} = 78.947 \ [r < k]$

When r = 12% $\quad P = \dfrac{10(0.75)}{0.12 - (0.25 \times 0.12)} = \dfrac{7.5}{0.09} = 83.33 \ [r = k]$

(i) Thus when the rate of return is greater than the cost of capital, the price per share increases with increase in the retention rate or decrease in the dividend payout ratio. In above illustration the price is ₹ 166.67 when the retention is 75% and ₹ 88.23 when the retention ratio is 25%.

(ii) When the rate of return is lower than the cost of capital of the company, it can improve the share price by increasing the dividend payout or conversely by decreasing the retention ratio. The price is ₹ 55.556 at 65% retention and ₹ 78.947 at 25% retention.

(iii) When the two rates are equal price remains constant irrespective of the dividend payout of the firm. In the example the price is ₹ 83.33 irrespective of whether the dividend policy is 75% retention or 25% retention ratio.

4.2.2 Irrelevance Theory of Dividend: Modigliani and Miller Model

According to the irrelevance theory of dividend, the dividend decisions of the company are irrelevant and hence dividend policy of the firm does not affect the value of the business. The shareholders substitute dividend for capital gain by selling the shares of the company. Further, every company has shareholders who agree with its dividend policy. Those who do not approve of the dividend policy of the firm leave it by selling their shares in the market.

Corporate Finance — Dividend Decisions

Hence the value of the business is dependent on the income generating capacity of the firm and the quality of its assets and not on the dividend policy. The MM model is based on the following assumptions:

1. There is no tax advantage or disadvantage associated with the dividends. Therefore shareholder's preference for capital gain or dividend is not dependent on tax policy.
2. Investment policy and dividend policy are not interlinked.
3. There are no flotation costs or transaction costs for raising funds from the capital market, so that company is indifferent between utilisation of retained earnings and issue of fresh shares for its funds requirement.
4. The future earnings of the firm are known with certainty.
5. The capital market is perfect. The cost of capital is constant.

According to the theory the total earning of the shareholders is the sum total of the capital appreciation and dividend. If the company pays dividend, the capital appreciation is less and if the company does not pay dividend the capital appreciation is such that it compensates for the amount of dividend the shareholders would have received had the company paid dividend.

The market price of the share of a firm is equal to the present value of the dividend at the end of the period plus the market price of the share at the end of the period.

Mathematical Formula

$$P = \frac{1}{1 + k_s}(D_1 + P_1)$$

P = Market price of the share at time 0
K_e = Cost of capital
D_1 = Dividend per share at time 1
P_1 = Market Price of share at time 1

Problem 4.6: ZTA Ltd. has 1,00,000 shares of ₹ 10 each. The current market price of the share is ₹ 120 per share. The cost of equity is 12%. Compute the expected market price of the share at the end of the year 1 –

(a) If dividend of ₹ 10 is paid; and
(b) If dividend is not paid at all.

Solution:

Given: $P_0 = 120$

$K_e = 12\%$ or 0.12

$D_1 = 10$

Substituting the figures in the MM Model of -

$$P = \frac{1}{1 + k_e}(D_1 + P_1), \text{ we get,}$$

$$120 = \frac{1}{1 + 0.12}(10 + P_1)$$

Or $(10 + P_1) = 120 \times 1.12$

Or $P_1 = 134.4 - 10$

$= 124.4$

When dividend is not paid

$$120 = \frac{1}{1 + 0.12}(0 + P_1)$$

Or $P_1 = 134.4 - 0 = 134.4$

When the company declares dividend, the market price ₹124. The total earnings of the shareholder consist of dividend plus the appreciation in the market price of share which is 10 + 4.4 = 14.4.

When the company does not declare dividend the total benefit of the shareholder is the appreciation in the market price of the share of the company which is 134.4 -120 = 14.4.

Thus the benefit to the shareholder is the same irrespective of the dividend policy of the firm.

Limitations of the MM Model

1. The assumption of absence of floatation cost is not true. Due to the existence of this cost a company cannot remain indifferent between raising funds from external sources and raising it internally through retained earnings. The floatation costs reduce the total proceeds from issue of shares.
2. The shareholders bear transaction cost. There is securities transaction tax (STT) as well. Hence sale of security involves cost to the shareholder whereas no such cost is applicable to dividend receipt. The net proceeds from sale of shares are reduced due to these costs. Therefore a shareholder will not find the capital gain revenue and revenue from dividend substitutable. The amount of dividend and capital gain are not equal.
3. Share prices fluctuate. The shareholders may find the income from capital gain to be uncertain and hence may prefer dividend to capital gain. Thus they are not indifferent between the two.
4. It has been assumed that the company can sell more shares in order to finance its activities at market price. But in actual practice companies offer additional shares at a price lower than the market price due to market compulsions. This makes retained earnings more valuable than dividend. Hence dividend policy is not irrelevant.

Corporate Finance — Dividend Decisions

5. Dividends are paid as they are given signals about the prosperity or otherwise of a company. If a company does not pay dividend or pays low amount of dividend, it may be taken as the management is uncertain about the future earnings of the company.

ILLUSTRATED PROBLEMS

Problem 4.7: From the following information of Xavier Ltd. compute price per share as per Walter's Model.

Face value of share ₹ 10
Rate of return required by the shareholders 12%
Rate of return on the investment generated by the company 16%
Earning per share ₹ 12
Payout ratio is 40%.

What will be the share price if company adopts a payout ratio of 50% and 60%?

Solution:

Earnings per share, (E) = ₹ 12
Dividend per share (D) when payout ratio is 40% [40% of 12] = ₹ 4.80
Dividend per share, (D) when payout ratio is 50% [50% of 12] = ₹ 6
Dividend per share (D) when payout ratio is 60% [60% of ₹ 12] = ₹ 7.20

Walter's model is –

$$P = \frac{D + \frac{r}{k}(E - D)}{k}$$

(i) With payout ratio of 40%

$$P = \frac{4.80 + \frac{0.16}{0.12}(12 - 4.80)}{0.12} = 120$$

(ii) When payout ratio is 50%

$$P = \frac{6 + \frac{0.16}{0.12}(12 - 6)}{0.12} = 116.67$$

(iii) When payout ratio is 60%

$$P = \frac{7.20 + \frac{0.16}{0.12}(12 - 7.20)}{0.12} = 113.33$$

The rate of earning of the firm is higher than the opportunity cost; the price of the share will increase as the payout is decreased. The share price is highest when the payout ratio is the lowest i.e., 40% of the earnings.

Problem 4.8: The following data is available from the records of Sultan Kher Ltd.

The net earnings of the company after tax are ₹ 80,00,000. Rate of return on investment is 15%. The cost of capital is 18%. Number of shares of the company is 10,00,000. The dividend payout ratio of the company is 25%.

What will be the price of the share as per the Gordon model of dividend theory? Will the market price change if the dividend payout ratio is changed to 60%, and if yes, how much?

Solution:

As per the Gordon Model the price of share of a company is given by the following formula:

$$P = \frac{E(1 - b)}{k - br}$$

$$E = \frac{80,00,000}{10,00,000} = ₹ 8$$

(a) Dividend payout ratio (1 – b) is 25% hence b is the reverse of dividend payout, i.e., b = 75%.

$$r = 0.15$$
$$k = 0.18$$
$$br = 0.75 \times 0.15 = 0.1125$$
$$P = \frac{8(0.25)}{0.18 - 0.1125} = 29.629$$

(b) Market price of share when dividend payout (1 – b) is 60%, b is 40%

$$r = 0.15$$
$$k = 0.18$$
$$br = 0.60 \times 0.15 = 0.09$$
$$P = \frac{8(0.60)}{0.18 - 0.09} = 53.33$$

In the case of this company r < k, hence as per Gordon's Model as the dividend payout is increased, the market price of the share increases. The market price of share is higher when the dividend payout is 60%.

The difference in the market price is 53.33 – 29.629 = 23.704.

Problem 4.9: Net Earnings of Piyush Ltd. for the year ending 2014 is ₹ 56,00,000. Using Walter's Model calculate the dividend payout rate, which will maximise the wealth of the shareholders? The expectation of shareholders is 18% and company's return on investment is 17%. Substantiate your answer. The number of shares outstanding is 7,00,000.

Solution: The cost of capital is 18% whereas the internal rate of return of the company is 17%, or r < k. In such a situation the optimum payout ratio would be to increase the dividend up to the maximum amount possible. Here it can be 100%. Applying Walter's model, the price of share can be calculated at – 100% payout ratio and at 0% payout ratio.

The mathematical formula for Walter's Model is

$$P = \frac{D + \frac{r}{k}(E - D)}{k}$$

$$E = \frac{56,00,000}{7,00,000} = 8$$

(i) When D is 100 % of Earnings per share:

$$D = 100\% \text{ of } ₹8 = 8$$
$$r = 0.17$$
$$k = 0.18$$

$$P = \frac{8 + \frac{0.17}{0.18}(8 - 8)}{0.18} = ₹44.44$$

(ii) When Dividend is 0% of Earnings per share

$$D = 0$$

$$P = \frac{0 + \frac{0.17}{0.18}(8 - 0)}{0.18} = 41.97$$

The share price is higher when the company adopts 100% payout ratio.

Problem 4.10: Compute the total earnings of Mr. Sohan Kapoor from the following details. He holds 500 shares of FBT Ltd., bought @ ₹ 45 per share a month ago. The company has decided to declare dividend at ₹ 9 per share out of an EPS of ₹ 12 per share. Company's return on investment is 16%. The cost of capitalisation is 18%.

Mr. Sohan sells his shares after receiving the dividend. Walter's Model holds for the company.

Solution: Total earnings of Sohan = Dividend + Capital gain on sale of shares

Dividend received = Dividend per share × Number of shares held

$$= 9 \times 500$$
$$= 4500$$

Capital gain = 500 (Sale price of each share – Purchase price of the share)

Market price of the share as per Walter's Model is given by the formula

$$P = \frac{D + \frac{r}{k}(E - D)}{k}$$

D = 9, E = 12, r = 0.16, k = 18%

$$P = \frac{9 + \frac{0.16}{0.18}(12 - 9)}{0.18} = 64.8167$$

Capital gain = 500 (64.8167 − 45)
= 9,908.35

Total earnings of Sohan = 4,500 + 9,908.35 = 14,408.35.

Problem 4.11: The following information about Krishna G. K. Ltd. is available:

Rate of return required by the shareholders is 16%.

EPS is ₹ 15

At what rate of return the market price of the share will be ₹ 150? Assume Gordon's model and dividend payout ratio of 40%.

Solution: The market price of share as per Gordon's model is given by the following formula:

$$P = \frac{E(1-b)}{k - br}$$

P = 150, E = 15, b = 0.60, (1 − b) = 0.40, k = 0.16, r = ?

$$150 = \frac{15(1 - 0.60)}{0.16 - 0.60r} \text{ or } 150 = \frac{15 \times 0.40}{0.16 - 0.6r}$$

(0.16 − 0.6r) = 0.04

Or − 0.6r = − 0.12

Or r = 0.2 or 20%

The internal rate of return of the company is 20%

Problem 4.12: The share capital of V Zed Ltd. consists of 25,000 shares of ₹ 100 each. The current earnings of the company is ₹ 2,00,000. Company is paying a dividend of ₹ 6 per share. Capitalisation rate applicable to the company is 10%. Assuming Gordon's Model, calculate the Price – Earning ratio.

Solution: Price earning ratio = $\frac{\text{Market price of share}}{\text{Earning per share}}$

As per Gordon's Model market price of share is given by the following formula

$$P = \frac{E(1-b)}{k - br}$$

$$E = \frac{2,00,000}{25,000} = 8$$

Retention ratio 'b' = (E − D)/E = $\frac{8 - 6}{8}$ = 0.25

Corporate Finance   Dividend Decisions

$$(1 - b) = (1 - 0.25) = 0.75$$

$$\text{Return on investment 'r'} = \frac{2,00,000}{25,00,000} = 0.08$$

$$K = 10\% \text{ or } 0.10$$

$$P = \frac{8(0.75)}{0.10 - (0.25 \times 0.08)} = 75$$

$$\text{Price Earning ratio} = \frac{75}{8} = 9.375.$$

Problem 4.13: ZEM Ltd. has 10,00,000 shares. The market price of the share is ₹ 100. The company is considering payment of ₹ 6 per share as dividend, at the end of the current year. The firm belongs to a risk class whose capitalisation rate is 10%. The company has a net income of ₹ 10,00,000. What will be the price after the dividend declaration? If dividend is not paid what will be the share price? MM model of dividend theory is applicable to the company.

Solution:

As per the MM model

$$P_0 = \frac{1}{1 + k_s}(D_1 + P_1)$$

P_0 = Current market price at time o = 100

$K_e = 10\%, D_1 = 6, P_1 = ?$

Applying the formula we get

$$100 = \frac{1}{1 + 0.10}(6 + P_1)$$

$$110 = 6 + P_1$$

$$P_1 = 110 - 6 = ₹ 104$$

The total benefit received by the shareholder is dividend of ₹ 6 and Share worth ₹ 104 i.e. ₹ 110.

According to the MM model, dividend decision is irrelevant. If the company does not pay dividend the price of the share at the end of the current year would be

$$100 = \frac{1}{1 + 0.10}(0 + P_1)$$

$$110 = P_1$$

The total benefit to the shareholder is ₹ 110, even when dividend is not declared.

Corporate Finance — Dividend Decisions

Problem 4.14: From the following information supplied, calculate the market price of the share both when dividend is declared by the company and when dividend is not declared by the company.

Price – Earning ratio = 10

Number of shares of the company = 5,00,000

Current market price of the share = ₹ 110 per share

Dividend to be paid at the end of the current year is ₹ 8 per share.

Net Earnings of the company for the year is ₹ 50,00,000.

Assuming MM model applies calculate the number of shares the company will have to issue in order to meet its investment requirement of ₹ 20,00,000.

Solution: As per MM model $P_o = \dfrac{1}{1 + k_s}(D_1 + P_1)$

$P_o = ₹ 110, D_1 = 8, P_1 = ? \; k_e = \dfrac{1}{P/E} = \dfrac{1}{10} = 0.10.$

(i) Market price of the share when dividend is paid

$$110 = \dfrac{1}{1 + 0.10}(8 + P_1)$$

$$121 - 8 = P_1$$

Market price after declaration of dividend ₹ 113

(ii) Market price of share when dividend is not paid

$$110 = \dfrac{1}{1 + 0.10}(0 + P_1)$$

$$P_1 = ₹ 121$$

(iii) Number of shares to be issued when dividend is declared

Amount available for investment = Net earnings – Dividend paid

$$= 50,00,000 - (8 \times 5,00,000)$$

$$= 10,00,000$$

The company's total requirement is ₹ 20,00,000. ₹ 10,00,000 or retained earning is available after dividend. It will require another ₹ 10,00,000 to finance its requirement. The company can raise the balance amount by issuing shares at the current market price which is ₹ 113.

Number of shares to be issued = $\dfrac{\text{Amount required}}{\text{Market price per share}} = \dfrac{10,00,000}{113} = 8,850$ shares

Points to Remember

- The word dividend is derived from the Latin word "dividendum", meaning things to be divided. The profits divided among the shareholders of a company is called dividend. It is expressed as a certain amount on each share or as a percentage on the market price of the share.
- Dividend is a distribution to shareholders out of profits or reserves available for the purpose.
- With respect to equity shareholders 'Dividend per Share' means the dividend payable per equity share. It is in the form of a certain amount. Dividends are declared normally as dividend per share, besides being expressed in the form of dividend yield.
- Dividend Pay-out Ratio is the ratio between the 'dividend per share' (DPS) and 'earning per share' (EPS) of a company. It indicates the part of earning of the company paid by way of dividend.
- Dividend Yield is the ratio of dividend per share and market price of the share. Investors are more interested to know as to how much their investment is earning for them.
- Dividend Cover shows the number of times the dividend to ordinary shareholders of a company is covered by the profit of the company after tax. It is calculated by dividing the net earnings of the company, by the dividend amount.
- Dividend Warrant is an instrument issued by a company to its registered shareholders stating the amount of dividend payable to the concerned shareholder asking the banker of the company to pay the specified amount to the shareholder or to his order.
- The policy of the management of a company regarding the division of its net earning between 'dividend to shareholders' and 'retained earning' is called the dividend policy.
- Important Consideration in Dividend Policy
    (a) Economy
    (b) Legal
    (c) Industry
    (d) Stability of dividend
    (e) Owner
    (f) Internal considerations
- According to Walter's Model, investment decision and dividend decisions of a firm are interlinked. The dividend decision of the firm influences the market price and the value of the firm when the rate of earning of the firm and the expected rate if earning of the shareholders are different.
- Gordon's theory of dividend policy favours the dividend relevance theory. It is based on the assumption that investors are risk averse, hence prefer current dividend to future dividend and capital appreciation. Future is uncertain both with regard to payment of dividend and timing of the payment. Hence as the retention ratio increases the investors discount the future earnings at a higher rate. They place lower value on the future earnings of the firm.

- According to the irrelevance theory of dividend, the dividend decisions of the company are irrelevant and hence dividend policy of the firm does not affect the value of the business. The shareholders substitute dividend for capital gain by selling the shares of the company.

Questions for Discussion

1. Explain the following concepts:
   (i) Dividend
   (ii) Dividend payout
   (iii) Dividend cover
   (iv) Dividend yield
   (v) Dividend per share
2. Explain the different types of Dividend.
3. Explain the factors that influence the Dividend policy of a company.
4. What are the assumptions of Walter's theory of dividend relevance? Does dividend payment by a company affect the market price of the share of the company? Explain with illustration.
5. Is the market price of a share same under Walter's and Gordon's model of dividend policy? Illustrate.
6. Compare the dividend models of Walter and Gordon.
7. What are the assumptions of the MM theory of dividend irrelevance?

Multiple Choice Questions

1. Rate of Dividend is recommended by
   (a) Equity shareholders
   (b) Shareholder
   (c) Board of Directors
   (d) Chief Financial Officer
2. Which of the following is not an assumption of MM Theory of Dividend Irrelevance?
   (a) No tax
   (b) Absence of floatation cost
   (c) No transaction cost
   (d) Imperfect capital market
3. Dividend payout ratio is the ratio of ......
   (a) Dividend per share and face value of share
   (b) Dividend per share and earnings per share
   (c) Market price and Dividend per share
   (d) Profit after tax and Dividend per share

Corporate Finance — Dividend Decisions

4. Dividend Relevance theory is advocated by ……
   (a) Walter and Miller
   (b) Walter and Modigliani
   (c) Miller and Modigliani
   (d) Walter and Gordon

5. Dividend is in the form of ……
   (a) Cash only
   (b) Cash and stock
   (c) Cash stock and property
   (d) Share only

6. Dividend payout is reciprocal of ……
   (a) Retention ratio
   (b) Price-Earnings ratio
   (c) Dividend-Yield
   (d) Dividend cover

7. Cost of equity share is ……
   (a) Reciprocal of price earnings ratio
   (b) Capitalisation rate of the risk class to which the firm belongs
   (c) It is the revenue expected by the equity shareholder
   (d) All the above

8. The formula for calculating the present value of an infinite stream of dividend is ……
   (a) $\dfrac{D}{k}$
   (b) $\dfrac{D}{1+k}$
   (c) $\dfrac{D}{1-k}$
   (d) $\dfrac{D+1}{k}$

9. As per the dividend relevance models, when k > r the company should ……
   (a) increase the dividend payout ratio to increase the wealth of the shareholders
   (b) decrease the payout ratio to increase the market price of the share
   (c) not pay any dividend
   (d) pay 100% dividend

10. Gordon's Model and Walter's Model of Dividend are applicable to firms that finance their activities through ……
    (a) equity only
    (b) net profits only
    (c) both equity and net earnings
    (d) only through debts

ANSWERS

1. (c)	2. (d)	3. (b)	4. (d)	5. (c)	6. (a)	7. (a)	8. (a)
9. (d)	10. (c)						

Corporate Finance — Dividend Decisions

Practical Problems

1. Suggest the best dividend payout ratio for a company under each of the different conditions following Walter's Model, from the following information.

   Earning per share is ₹ 20 and the rate of capitalisation applicable to the company is 12%. The company earns a. 15%; b. 10%; c. 12% on its investment.

   The dividend payout options available to the company are – (a) 50%, (b) 75%, (c) 100%.

   [Answer: At 15% return 50% dividend payout is best with 187.50 at 10%, 100% dividend payout ₹ 166.67, at 12% all payouts give the same price i.e. 166.67]

2. Xavier's Ltd. has 8 lakh equity shares outstanding at the beginning of the year 2013. The current market price of equity share is ₹ 120 per share. The board of directors of the company is contemplating ₹ 6.40 per share to be paid as dividend. The rate of capitalisation, appropriate to the risk class to which the company belongs is 9.6%.

   (a) Based on the MM approach, calculate the market price of the share of the company, when the dividend is declared and also when it is not declared.

   (b) How many new shares are to be issued by the company if the company desires to fund an investment project requiring a ₹ 3.20 crores by the end of the year assuming one income for the year will be ₹ 1.60 crores? Assume dividend is declared.

   [Answer: (a) 125.12, 131.52, (b) 1,68,798]

3. From the following information supplied to you comment if the D/P ratio of the firm is optimum as per Walter's model.

30,000 shares of ₹ 100 each	₹ 30,00,000
Net earnings of the company	4,50,000
Dividend paid	2,40,000
Price earning ratio	12.5%

   What should be the price earning ratio, so that the market price is not affected?

   [Answer: k = 1/Price – Earning i.e. 8%, r = Net earnings/Share capital 15%, P = 264.0625, Not optimum, since r > k 0% dividend is best at which P is 351.5625, when k = r price is not affected i.e. P/E ratio of 15 times].

   ✳✳✳

Chapter 5...

Corporate Restructuring

Contents ...

- 5.1 Corporate Restructuring
  - 5.1.1 Meaning of Corporate Restructuring
  - 5.1.2 Features of Corporate Restructuring
  - 5.1.3 Reasons for Corporate Restructuring
  - 5.1.4 Broad Areas of Restructure
- 5.2 Techniques of Restructuring
  - 5.2.1 Expansion Techniques
  - 5.2.2 Disinvestment
  - 5.2.3 Other Techniques
- 5.3 Strategies of Restructuring
- Points to Remember
- Questions for Discussion
- Multiple Choice Questions
- Project Questions

Learning Objectives...

- To understand the concept of corporate restructuring
- To know the reasons for corporate restructuring
- To study the broad areas of corporate restructuring
- To be able to explain the techniques of corporate restructuring

5.1 Corporate Restructuring

5.1.1 Meaning of Corporate Restructuring

We hear about splitting of giant companies like Reliance, disinvestment of shares of the government in the public sector undertaking like Coal India, proposals about merger state units of big banks like SBI branches etc. These events are called as 'Restructuring'. 'Corporate Restructuring' is a process of redesigning one or more aspects of a company in order to make it more profitable and effective. These aspects include ownership pattern, business operations, capital structure, technology, legal form of organisation etc. It may be noted that these events do not occur in the normal course of business, rather are conscious choices made by the management of organisation with clear cut motives. 'Corporate Restructuring' results in significant expansion, contraction or change in the business activity which has impact on the profitability and continuity of business of a company. Small changes made in the organisations are not restructuring, they are just 'organisational change'.

According **to Crum and Goldberg,** *"Restructuring of a company is a set of discrete decisive measure taken in order to increase the competitiveness of the enterprise and thereby to enhance its value".*

The dictionary meaning as per **Oxford Dictionary** of Business and Management is "a change in the 'business strategy' of a company by diversification into new areas, which it considers more attractive. Alternatively, following poor performance, it may seek to withdraw from an area by divestment or closure of parts of its business, which it no longer considers part of its future strategic focus.

5.1.2 Features of Corporate Restructuring

1. It is a one time transaction based on the conscious decision of the management of a company. It is not a change in the ordinary course of business.
2. It affects the future cash flows of the company. It has long run impact.
3. It involves significant change in the strategy of a company - Financial, operational, organisational or technological strategies.
4. There may be more than one reason for restructuring besides profit making, like reviving a sick unit, diversification, market penetration, dealing with new government policies etc.
5. It may involve change in the form of organisation, ownership and control, management, business operation, debt-equity ratio etc.
6. There are legal formalities involved in corporate restructures in the form of agreements, communication to Registrar of companies etc. and in some cases government regulations have to be faced as is in the case of 'takeover'.

5.1.3 Reasons for Corporate Restructuring

Corporate restructuring affects a company, its management, investors and employees significantly. Hence the management and promoters of the company have to be very clear about the reasons for restructuring. Further an analysis of the reasons would guide the company in the choice of the best technique of restructuring.

A company may go for restructuring for one or more of the following reasons:

1. **Expansion and Growth:** One of the main reasons for amalgamation and acquisitions is to expand the operation of the company and increase the growth rate. Instead of working to expand within, it is less time consuming to expand by mergers and acquisitions.

2. **Competitive:** A company may go for restructuring in order to make it more competitive as compared to other firms in the industry. Joint ventures, technological collaborations, marketing arrangements etc. may be resorted to for the purpose.

3. **Leverage:** If a company is highly leveraged i.e., its capital structure contains high ratio of debt, it may go for financial restructure to increase the proportion of equity and thereby reduce its interest burden.

4. **Economies of Scale:** It may go for mergers, acquisition, purchase of divisions etc. to enjoy economies of large scale production and reduce the cost of operations.

5. **Unutilised Capacity:** If a company has unutilised capacities, it may go for restructuring to utilise the excess capacity.

6. **Market Price of Share:** A company may resort to restructuring if its shares are undervalued as represented by its market price.

7. **Concentration:** A company which is diversified may demerge or divestiture one or more of its divisions in order to focus on core business activity.

8. **Government Policies:** Firms may be required by Government policies to go for restructuring to adapt itself to changed environment.

9. **Business Cycles:** Economic cycles may force firms to consolidate or diversify their business operations. It has been observed that during recession, industries try to be more effective through consolidation and spin-offs and in times of prosperity through takeovers and acquisitions.

10. **Independence:** In order to reduce their dependence on suppliers of raw material, stores, spare parts etc. companies may restructure in the form of mergers and acquisitions with the supplier firms.

11. **Market Penetration:** A company in need to market its products intensively in the same market may go for business alliances, outsourcing, licensing etc.

12. **Market Leadership:** A company aiming at becoming market leader may go for horizontal merger, acquisition of companies dealing in same or similar products, may go for hostile takeover bids.

13. **Risk Reduction:** Company operating exposed to high business risk may like to share the risk by business alliances, by selling of a part of its business or a unit of a business to another company.

14. **Deal with Competition:** To manage competition from other organisations, alliances, mergers with the competitor or acquiring another company may be resorted to. Increase in size of a company can help in dealing with competition.

5.1.4 Broad Areas of Restructure

Areas of restructure include:

1. **Ownership and Control:** Equity shareholders are the real owners of a company as they have voting rights and are entitled to all the residual. A significant change in the debt-equity proportions in the capital of a company changes the ownership and control. Issue of debt, buy-back of shares, conversion of debt into equity etc. are some examples.

2. **Management:** Change in the composition of board of directors, change in organisational structure, span of control, redesigning of boundaries of the departments of an organisations are examples of change in the management. Amalgamations, acquisitions, and takeovers can cause significant change in the management of a company.

3. **Business Operations:** A company may change its product line or market segment, by increasing the nature and quantity of products produced by it. Diversification and expansion, acquisition, demergers and collaboration may cause a significant change in the products produced and market accessed by companies.

4. **Technology:** Companies can use latest technologies of production, process, marketing etc. by investing huge amounts in R&D and by way of strategic alliances with the overseas companies.

5.2 Techniques of Restructuring

Techniques of restructuring are shown below in Fig. 5.1.

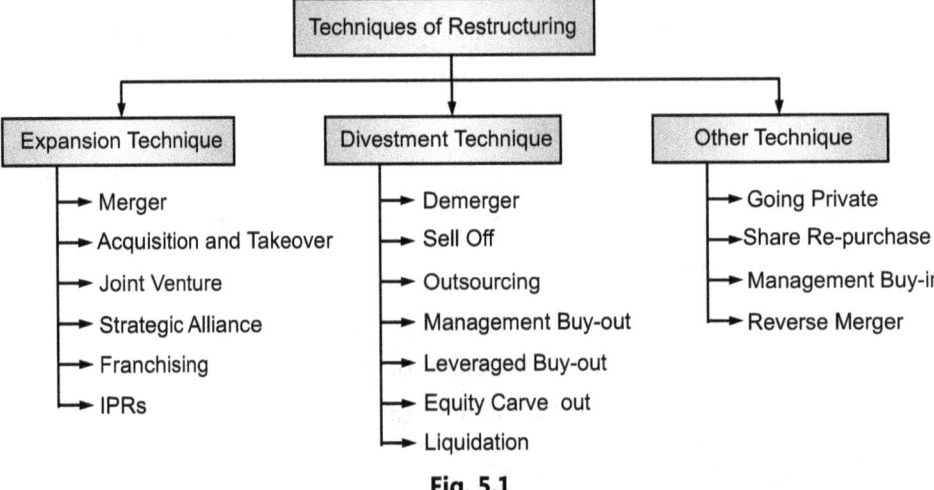

Fig. 5.1

5.2.1 Expansion Techniques

It is increase in the existing capacity of a business by increasing capital investment and assets purchase.

1. **Mergers and Amalgamation**

    Merger or amalgamation is the combining of two or more companies into one. It may take place by absorption or consolidation. IT Act 1961 defines *"Amalgamation means the merger of one or more companies with another company or companies to form one company, in such a manner that, it results in:*

    - *Transfer of all properties and liabilities of amalgamating companies to the amalgamated company; and*
    - *Shareholders holding not less than $3/4^{th}$ in value of the shares of the amalgamating companies would become the shareholders of the amalgamated company."*

    Amalgamation may take place by absorption or consolidation.

    (a) Under **absorption** one company takes over the assets and liabilities of one or more companies and pays the shareholders of the absorbed company or companies, shares of the absorbing company. The companies that are being absorbed close.

    (b) **Consolidation** is a method of merger, where two or more companies wind up and form into a new company. The assets and liabilities of the amalgamating company are taken over by a new company. The shareholders of the old company are given the shares of the newly formed company.

Types of Mergers: Mergers can be of the following types:

(a) **Horizontal Merger:** It is the merger of two or more companies in the same line of business. Horizontal merger results in economies of scale, operating economies and elimination of competition. It creates sometimes concentration of economic power hence is controlled by regulations.

(b) **Vertical Merger:** This is the merger of two or more companies involved in different stages of production or distribution of the same product or service. Vertical merger creates forward and backward linkages. An automobile company merging with a tyre producing company and a warehousing company is an example of such mergers.

(c) **Conglomerate Merger:** It involves the merger of two or more companies whose businesses are not related. Such a merger results in diversification of activities.

(d) **Reverse Merger:** In a reverse merger, a profit making company mergers with a loss making business or a financially weak business. The healthy company is dissolved. The advantage of such merger is the merged company can show less profit or carry over the losses and thereby reduce tax burden.

(e) **Cross Border Merger:** It involves the merger and acquisition of firms belonging to two different countries of the world. Such mergers give access to latest technology and expanded market, access to large capital market, and trading of the shares of the company in more than one country.

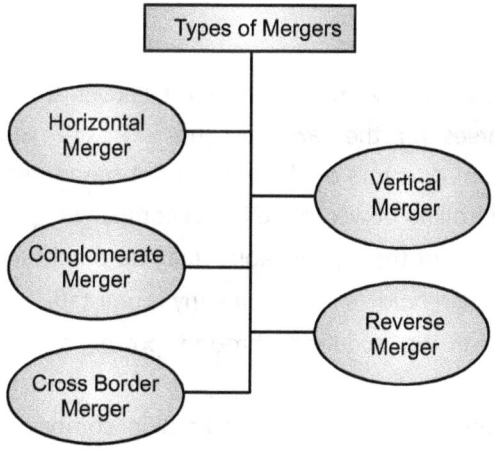

Fig. 5.2

Synergies/Benefits of Mergers

(a) **Economies of Large Scale:** Merger results in increasing the size of operations of the company. The merged company enjoys economies of large scale resulting from reduction in the average cost- both production and distribution cost.

(b) **Finance:** Mergers increases the capital base of the company and also increase its access to further capital in future.

(c) **Efficient Management:** The merged company can afford highly trained management personnel.

(d) **Access to Latest Technology:** Due to better finances and large scale operations, the merged company can avail latest technology in its operations.

Limitations or Dangers of Mergers

(a) Healthy competition may get eliminated due to mergers.

(b) It may result in concentration of economic power.

(c) It may reduce the performance of the merged company.

2. Acquisition and Takeover

Acquisition is the acquiring of another company by purchasing its assets and liabilities or by acquiring the controlling power in the company. The control may be acquired by purchase of the majority of the shares carrying voting rights or controlling the composition of the board of directors. The purchase of a certain block of Equity Share capital of a company results in transferring the controlling power into the hands of the purchaser. The controlling power can be acquired if more than 50% of the shares are held by acquirer. Practically, acquisition of a smaller percentage of equity share capital gets the power of control as a large part of the share capital might be held by large number of scattered shareholders.

Ways of Acquiring Control

The takeover can be a friendly one or a hostile takeover. It is a friendly takeover when the target company agrees for the takeover and is hostile when the takeover bid is unwelcome to the board of directors or shareholders of the target company. Following are the ways of acquiring controlling power in the target company:

(a) Substantial portion of the equity capital may be purchased in the stock market or from individual shareholders if the company is unlisted.

(b) Voting rights can be acquired through power of attorney or proxy voting arrangements.

(c) By acquiring control over an Investor holding company which holds controlling interest in the target company. It is an indirect way of acquisition.

Hostile Takeover

Techniques: A company intending to takeover can use any of the following techniques to takeover the target company:

1. **Street Sweep:** As per this technique the acquirer accumulates large amounts of stock in the target company before making open offer. This leaves the target company with no option but to agree to the takeover bid.
2. **Strategic alliance:** It is an offer of partnership. The acquirer can exercise control after becoming a member in the target company.
3. **Bear Hug:** The acquirer threatens to make an offer and pressurises the board to agree for settlement or change of control.
4. **Brand Power:** The target company is put in a weak position by entering into alliance with powerful brands.

Defences against Hostile Takeovers

In order to defend against a hostile takeover bid against a company, some of the following methods are adopted:

1. **Preferential Allotment:** Corporate make preferential allotment of equity shares to the promoter group to increase the equity held by it.
2. **Poison Pill:** Company can issue low price shares to its existing shareholders to enlarge the capital base. This would make hostile takeover too expensive.
3. **Greenmail:** As per this strategy, the target company repurchases the shares cornered by the potential acquirer and allow them to make profit in the deal.
4. **Amalgamation** of two or more companies promoted by the same group.
5. **Pac-man defence:** As per this strategy, the target company makes counter bid for the raider company.
   If the takeover bid is understood to be due to some of the **assets** owned by the company, then company may sell of those assets in order to make it less attractive for takeover.
6. **White Knight**: It may take support from its friends and ask them not to sell their shares if they already have, and to purchase the shares of the company if they do not own shares of the company. This will reduce the proportion of shares available for takeover hence making the takeover ineffective. Besides, the friendly company won't interfere in the management.

SEBI Guidelines for Substantial Acquisition and Control

In order to protect the interest of company and investors SEBI has issued guidelines for acquisition of shares in the target company. The following rules are the extract from the guidelines.

(a) No acquirer shall acquire shares or voting rights in a target company which taken together with shares or voting rights, if any, held by him and by persons acting in concert with him in such target company, entitle them to exercise **twenty-five per** cent or more of the voting rights in such target company unless the acquirer makes a public announcement of an open offer for acquiring shares of such target company in accordance with these regulations.

(b) No acquirer, who together with persons acting in concert with him, has acquired and holds in accordance with these regulations shares or voting rights in a target company entitling them to exercise twenty-five per cent or more of the voting rights in the target company but less than the maximum permissible non-public shareholding, shall acquire within any financial year **additional shares or voting rights in such target company entitling them to exercise more than five per cent** of the voting rights, unless the acquirer makes a public announcement of an open offer for acquiring shares of such target company in accordance with these regulations:

Provided that such acquirer shall not be entitled to acquire or enter into any agreement to acquire shares or voting rights exceeding such number of shares as would take the aggregate shareholding pursuant to the acquisition above the maximum permissible non-public shareholding.

Explanation: For purposes of determining the quantum of acquisition of additional voting rights under this sub-regulation –

(i) Gross acquisitions alone shall be taken into account regardless of any intermittent fall in shareholding or voting rights whether owing to disposal of shares held or dilution of voting rights owing to fresh issue of shares by the target company.

(ii) In the case of acquisition of shares by way of issue of new shares by the target company or where the target company has made an issue of new shares in any given financial year, the difference between the pre-allotment and the post-allotment percentage voting rights shall be regarded as the quantum of additional acquisition.

(iii) For the purposes of sub-regulation (1) and sub-regulation (2), acquisition of shares by any person, such that the individual shareholding of such person acquiring shares exceeds the stipulated thresholds, shall also be attracting the obligation to make an open offer for acquiring shares of the target company irrespective of whether there is a change in the aggregate shareholding with persons acting in concert.

(iv) Irrespective of acquisition or holding of shares or voting rights in a target company, no acquirer shall acquire, directly or indirectly, control over such target company unless the acquirer makes a public announcement of an open offer for acquiring shares of such target company in accordance with these regulations.

3. Business Alliance

These are limited period or purpose arrangements with other companies for use of technology, access to new markets etc. Alliances are based on one time agreement between the two or more companies. Business alliances are in the form of joint ventures, strategic alliances, equity partnership, franchising, licensing, and network alliances. Business alliances may be resorted to by companies to reduce risk and share gain, reduce cost, access new markets or for favourable regulatory treatment.

(a) **Joint Ventures**: It is an arrangement where two or more organisations participate collectively as a separate legal entity. The participating organisations enter into joint venture agreement stating the ownership rights, the profit division among the members, the risk sharing among them, and the operational responsibility of the participating companies. It is one time venture. Once the venture objective is attained, the members get separate.

(b) **Strategic Alliances:** Under this arrangement two or more companies may agree to transfer technology, provide R&D service, share marketing rights etc. the companies do not form into a separate legal entity.

(c) **Equity Partnership:** When in a strategic alliance one company takes minority stake in the equity of another, it is a case of equity partnership.

(d) **Licensing:** Under this method of business alliance, license agreement is entered into for obtaining a specific technology, producing a particular product or using a particular process, trade mark or copyright from the owner company. It is time bound, but can be renewed if agreement provides for it.

(e) **Franchise alliance:** Franchise to sell goods and service of a company can be obtained.

(f) **Network alliance:** In multimedia, computer, airline and telecommunications industries network alliance is entered into to use a particular route, web, or tower etc. normally it is entered into companies operating in different geographical areas.

Advantages of Business Alliances

1. It is difficult to develop a new technology. It requires lot of funds and time to do so. A business alliance with a company which has already developed the technology is a better option in the sense the time and effort is saved.

2. Business risks are high in this competitive global economy. Business alliances help in sharing the risks associated with production, application of new technology, accessing new market etc.
3. The regulations on business alliances are less stringent as compared to those on mergers, acquisitions and takeovers.
4. Due to economies of large scale and sharing of manufacturing facilities cost can be reduced.
5. Mergers, acquisitions, and takeovers are hard on employees of an organisation since they may face new culture, rules, policies, new management etc. But business alliances cause much less changes in organisation.

5.2.2 Disinvestment

It is the process of sale of assets or a unit of an organisation by way of sale of assets at market value or liquidation price or by sale of all or majority of the voting stock of a company. It may take the following forms:

1. **Divestiture or Demerger:** It involves the sale of a division or plant or unit of one company to another. For the seller it is a form of contraction of business and from the buyer's point of view, it is expansion. The selling company's liquidity position improves due to such sale. One of the important purposes of divestiture is to raise funds. If the unit which is sold was earning subnormal profit or was making loss, then divestiture cuts the losses of the company. A company might sell off a unit which is unrelated to its line of business. Sale helps a company concentrate on the other unit. Demerger is thus opposite of merger. It is the sale of one or more undertakings of a company to another company. The company making such a sale is called the demerged company and the undertaking in whose favour such a transfer is made is the resulting company. A demerger may take place in the form of a spin-off or a split-up.
    (i) **Spin off:** Under this arrangement the product line of a company or an undertaking of the company is reorganised into a separate entity either in the form of a subsidiary company or altogether a separate company.
    (ii) **Split-up:** Under a split-up arrangement, a company is split up into two or more independent companies. The parent company no more exists, in its place two or more companies emerge.
2. **Asset Sale:** It is the sale of certain assets of a company to another. Sale of assets related to a particular product line, reduces the burden of the company. Selling company can concentrate on the other product lines and business operations.

3. **Hive off:** It is the sale of a loss making division or product line by a diversified company. It enables the selling company to get rid of a difficult business and concentrate on profitable business segments.

4. **Leveraged Buy-outs (LBO):** Under a leveraged buyout a division or unit of a company is bought primarily with debt finance. When purchasers have limited financial capacity to invest in such a transaction, they may approach financial institutions, investors, venture funds, banks etc. for debt financing. Therefore the debt proportion is higher than the proportion of equity finance in such transactions.

   According to '**Emery and Finnerty**', a leveraged buyout is an acquisition that is financed principally sometimes more than 90%, by borrowing on a secured basis. The financial risk increases hence firms try to keep their operating leverages lower. The success of buyout depends on the future performance of the unit. If the sponsors of the unit succeed in controlling cost and improve the performance of the unit, then the interest on the debt and principal repayment can be met out of the cash flows of the operations. Otherwise, the interest cost will prove to be a burden.

5. **Outsourcing:** A firm may follow this strategy sometimes. In this strategy, some of the existing functions of a firm may be outsourced in the sense; they may be given to an outside agency. Agreed service charges are required to be paid for rendering these services. A firm may outsource its functions as part of cost control and cost reduction. For example, a firm may decide that accounting function may be outsourced to outside firm on payment of certain service charges. In such situation, the outsourcing firm will not be required to maintain its staff. All that it will be required is to pay the service charges to the service provider. A firm may decide to outsource some other functions such as human resources management, after sale service and repair and maintenance.

6. **Management buy outs:** The acquisition of a company by the management of an organisation is called management buy-out. It is carried out by a firm of management consultants who specialise in this type of review. The review will cover all aspects of running the organisation.

7. **Equity Carve-out:** It is the offering of a full or partial interest in a subsidiary to the public. It is like an IPO of a corporate subsidiary or a split-off IPO. This method of restructuring creates a new publicly traded company with partial or complete autonomy from the parent company. It is different from spin off in the following ways:

   (a) In spin-off shares of spun company are distributed to the existing shareholders of the parent company, whereas in equity carve-out the shares of the new company are sold to the new investors.

(b) Equity carve-out results in cash infusion to the parent company, whereas spin off does not result in such cash infusion.

8. **Liquidation:** It is closing down of a company. The assets of the company are sold away and liabilities are paid out of the proceeds. Any residual amount is distributed to the shareholders of the company.

5.2.3 Other Techniques

1. **Privatisation:** Privatisation involves transfer of ownership, partial or total of public enterprises from the government to individuals and non-governmental institutions. It involves the disinvestment of equity shares in the PSU by the government.

2. **Share Repurchase or Buy-Back:** It is a programme by which a company purchases its own shares from its shareholders. The repurchased shares may be cancelled or kept for reissue later. The reduction in the outstanding shares of the company causes an increase in the EPS. Company may follow any of the following methods to buy-back-

    (a) **Purchase from the Market:** Under this method company purchase the required number of share from the stock exchange at the prevailing market price.

    (b) **Purchase by Tender Offer:** Company may fix the price at which it intends to buy the shares of the company. The interested shareholders can tender their shares for re-purchase.

    (c) **Book-building Method:** Under this method company decides the price range for the shares repurchase. Shareholders are invited to tender their shares at any price within the stated price range. Company analyses the demand price and selects the lowest price offered for the required number of shares for buy-back. It pays all those who have offered their shares at that price or lower than that price.

3. **Leveraged Re-capitalisation:** Under this strategy a company takes significant amount of additional debt in order to pay large cash dividends to its shareholders or to buy its own shares. In either case, the proportion of equity is reduced and that of borrowings or debt is increased. It is often used as an anti-takeover measure i.e. to ward off potential acquirers from hostile takeover of the corporate.

4. **Reverse Merger**: In a reverse merger, a profit making company merges with a loss making business or a financially weak business. The healthy company is dissolved. The advantage of such merger is the merged company can show less profit or carry over the losses and thereby reduce tax burden.

5. **Slump Sale**: In a slump sale, a company disposes off the whole or substantially the whole of its undertaking for a lump-sum consideration. Values are not assigned to

individual assets and liabilities. A business transfer agreement is entered between the parties which states the terms and conditions of sale. The purchase price agreed for the transfer of assets and liabilities is called the 'slump price'.

6. **Management buy-in:** The acquisition of a company by an outside team of managers, specially formed for the purpose is management buy in. Such transactions are usually backed by venture-capital organisation.

7. **Debt Equity Swap:** A company which finds it difficult to repay its debt and to pay the interest on the debt might resort to convert its debt into equity. This conversion is called as debt equity swap

5.3 Strategies of Restructuring

Strategy is a plan of action. Restructuring require strategies at three levels:

(a) **Corporate strategy:** It is concerned with overall purpose and is known as grand strategy or root strategy.

(b) **Business strategy:** It is derived from the grand strategy and is directly concerned with the plans for profits.

(c) **Operational strategy:** It is the breaking down of the business plans into plans of actions at the operating level.

A company may go for the restructuring only after analysis of its present position and future expectations. Depending on the requirement it can go for any one of more of the following restructuring plans:

1. **Portfolio Restructuring**

Portfolio restructuring involves significant changes in the mix of assets owned by a firm or the lines of business operations. It takes the form of – divestitures, asset sales, spin-offs and liquidation. Portfolio restructuring helps to sharpen the company's focus on the core division.

2. **Financial Restructuring**

It is a significant change in the financial structure of the company and / or the pattern of ownership and control. It includes leveraged buy-outs, leveraged re-capitalisation and debt for equity swaps.

According to Donaldson, "the elements of the corporate structure include the:

- Scale of investment base,
- The mix between active investment and defensive reserve,
- The focus of investment (choice of revenue source),
- The rate at which earnings are re-invested,

- The mix of debt and equity contracts,
- The nature, degree and cost of corporate overhead,
- The distribution of expenditure between current and future revenue potential and the nature and duration of wage and benefit contracts".

3. Organisational Restructuring

It involves a significant change in the organisational structure of the firm. Such as redesigning divisional boundaries, flattening of hierarchal level, spreading of the span of control, reducing diversification, revising employee compensation, downsizing employment, better governance. Common types of organisational restructuring include the following:

(a) **Regrouping of business units:** It involves the regrouping of the existing business units into few strategic profit centres. The responsibility of performance is transferred to each group so formed.

(b) **Centralisation/Decentralisation:** Some units or functions of organisation may be centralised to have effective control and to facilitate flow of information through right channels so that only the necessary information reaches the highest level managers after filtering of unnecessary ones.

Large organisations go for decentralisation to reduce the delay in decision-making, communication, and efficiency. It reduces the length of the organisational structure.

(c) **Training and Deployment:** Training enables the work force to cope with the changing environment. Some employees may need deployment.

(d) **Downsizing:** In order to cut cost a company may adopt retrenchment of excess employees.

(e) **Changing HR policies:** HR policies concerning recruitment, selection, promotion, demotion, transfer, retirement, facilities like canteen etc. may be changed to suit the requirement of the company.

(f) **Pay structure:** The incentive and compensation plans may be changed to motivate the employees and also to cut cost.

(g) **Engineering:** The process of production, distribution etc. may be changed to improve performance.

Points to Remember

- **Restructuring** of a company is a set of discrete decisive measure taken in order to increase the competitiveness of the enterprise and thereby to enhance its value.
- **Merger or amalgamation** is the combining of two or more companies into one.

- Under absorption one company takes over the assets and liabilities of one or more companies and pays the shareholders of the absorbed company or companies, shares of the absorbing company. The companies that are being absorbed close.
- **Consolidation** is a method of merger, where two or more companies wind up and form into a new company. The assets and liabilities of the amalgamating company are taken over by a new company. The shareholders of the old company are given the shares of the newly formed company.
- **Acquisition** is the acquiring of another company by purchasing its assets and liabilities or by acquiring the controlling power in the company. The control may be acquired by purchase of the majority of the shares carrying voting rights or controlling the composition of the board of directors.
- **Business Alliances** are limited period or purpose arrangements with other companies for use of technology, access to new markets etc.
- **Disinvestment** is the process of sale of assets or a unit of an organisation by way of sale of assets at market value or liquidation price or by sale of all or majority of the voting stock of a company.
- **Divestiture or demerger** involves the sale of a division or plant or unit of one company to another.
- Hive off is the sale of a loss making division or product line by a diversified company.
- Under a leveraged buyout a division or unit of a company is bought primarily with debt finance.
- In outsourcing strategy, some of the existing functions of a firm may be outsourced in the sense; they may be given to an outside agency.
- **Acquisition** of a company by the management of an organisation is called management buy-out.
- **Liquidation** is closing down of a company. The assets of the company are sold away and liabilities are paid out of the proceeds.
- **Portfolio restructuring** involves significant changes in the mix of assets owned by a firm or the lines of business operations.
- **Financial Restructuring** is a significant change in the financial structure of the company and / or the pattern of ownership and control.
- **Organisational Restructuring** involves a significant change in the organisational structure of the firm.

Questions for Discussion

1. Differentiate spin off and split up
2. What is takeover? What are the defences against hostile takeover bids?
3. What are the advantages and disadvantages of mergers and acquisitions?
4. Define restructuring. What are the reasons of restructuring?
5. What is Corporate Restructuring? What are the broad areas of restructuring? Explain in brief the techniques of corporate restructuring.
6. What is amalgamation? Explain the types of Mergers. What are the advantages and disadvantages of mergers?

Multiple Choice Questions

1. Re-organisation of a product line of a company into a separate entity is ......
   (a) Spin-off
   (b) Split up
   (c) Demerger
   (d) Acquisition

2. When a unit of a company is bought primarily with debt finance it is ......
   (a) Acquisition
   (b) Leveraged capitalisation
   (c) LBO
   (d) Buy-back

3. Under vertical merger two or more companies ......
   (a) Having same product line are merged
   (b) Having different product lines are merged
   (c) Involved in different stages of production are merged
   (d) Situated in different countries are merged

4. Franchise is a type of ......
   (a) Business alliance
   (b) Financial restructuring
   (c) Organisational restructuring
   (d) Portfolio restructuring

5. Buy-back of own share by a company results in ......
   (a) Cash infusion
   (b) Reduction in outstanding shares
   (c) Increase in the EPS
   (d) (b) and (c) above

6. Portfolio restructuring acquiring company has to make an open offer to the public if the acquisition leads to exercise of ……
   (a) equal to or more than 20 % of the voting rights
   (b) more than 15% of the voting rights
   (c) more than 5 % of the voting rights
   (d) more than 25% of the voting rights
7. The parent company under a restructuring plan is divided into two or more companies, and loses its identity ……
   (a) Spin off (b) Demerger
   (c) Divestiture (d) Split up

ANSWERS

| 1. (a) | 2. (c) | 3. (c) | 4. (a) | 5. (d) | 6. (d) | 7. (d) |

Project Questions

1. 'Corporate restructuring can prove to be a double-edged sword.' Comment.
2. 'Strategic alliances can help shape what an industry may look like in the future.' Discuss.

***

Case Study

Case 1: Corporate Restructuring in India: A Case Study of Reliance Industries Limited (RIL)

In the current scenario restructuring has become the need of the hour for any organization to survive. Reliance Industries Limited (RIL). For example, the acquisition, merger, and demerger of Reliance Industries Ltd. like their acquisition of IPCL mergers of Reliance Petrochemicals Ltd., and the recent demergers of four entities like Reliance Communication Ventures Ltd., Reliance Energy Ventures Ltd., Reliance Natural Resources Ventures Ltd., and Reliance Capital Ventures Ltd. which spun off from Reliance Industries Ltd. (RIL), and were perhaps the most well-known restructurings in current times. RIL entered into the telecom sector in the year 2000. It also intended to combine its finance company with another subsidiary Reliance Petrochemicals Ltd. (RPL). In March 2002, RPL amalgamated with RIL. RIL also bagged a 25 percent share of IPCL in the same year. After the RIL patriarch Dhirubai Ambani passed away, RIL branched out further into the areas of biotech, life sciences, mining, and insurance.

Division of Reliance

RIL split in June 2005 due to issues between the two successors. The RIL struggle was not only a conflict of titans, but it was also about wealth in the area of ₹ 1000 billion which was not uncomplicated to distribute. On January 17th 2006, a unique trading and investment era was over. The demerger permitted by RIL board in August 2005, both brothers, Mukesh and Anil–directed different businesses and five listed companies emerged as potential investment opportunities for investors by March 2006. Among the group companies of RIL, Reliance Energy and Reliance Capital, were already listed at the exchanges. The remaining four companies were listed by the end of March 2006.

Current Structure

The new RIL structure gave Mukesh absolute independent control in the business of oil exploration, refining, petrochemicals, and textile businesses through a standalone entity in RIL along with IPCL. His shares also included biotech firm Reliance Life Sciences and Trevira, a company in Europe which manufactures polyester fibres. Anil got control over power, communication, and financial businesses through four companies which came under Anil Dhirubhai Ambani Enterprise (ADAE) as part of the Reliance group. These four companies were named as Reliance Capital Ventures Ltd. (pro-posed to be merged with another listed company Reliance Capital Ltd.), Reliance Energy Ventures Ltd. (proposed to be merged with existing company Reliance Energy Ltd.), Reliance Communication Ventures Ltd. (these include both Reliance Infocomm and Reliance Telecom) and Reliance Natural Resources Ltd. (which includes businesses in gas based energy undertakings).

Impact of the Demerger

Share prices of the listed five companies were cited differently at the Bombay Stock Exchange and National Stock Exchange after the Demerger. Before the split, RIL's share was traded around ₹ 978 per share, but after the demerger the united demerged share values of five companies came to around ₹ 1235. This was an increase of nearly 26 percent for each shareholder. Long term aspect of the demerger sill needs to studied.

Questions

1. What is the type of corporate restructuring adopted by Reliance in the year 2005?
2. What are the reasons for restructuring?
3. Name the areas of restructuring.
4. What are the impacts of restructuring?

***

Case 2: Corporate Governance at Infosys

By the late 1990s, Infosys Technologies Limited (Infosys) had clearly emerged as one of the best managed companies in India. Its corporate governance practices seemed to be better than those of many other companies in India. Because of its good governance practices, Infosys was the recipient of many awards. In 2001, Infosys was rated India's most respected company by Business World. Infosys was also ranked second in corporate governance among 495 emerging companies in a survey conducted by Credit Lyonnais Securities Asia (CLSA) Emerging Markets. It was voted India's best managed company five years in a row (1996-2000) by the Asiamoney poll. In 2000, Infosys had been awarded the "National Award for Excellence in Corporate Governance" by the Government of India. In 1999, Infosys had been selected as one of Asia's leading companies in the Far Eastern Economic Review's REVIEW 2000 Survey and voted India's most admired company by The Economic Times. Infosys had also provided all the information required by the Cadbury committee Infosys had benchmarked its corporate governance practices against those of the best managed companies in the world.

It was one of the first companies in India to publish a compliance report on corporate governance, based on the recommendations of a committee constituted by the Confederation of Indian Industries (CII). Infosys maintained a high degree of transparency

Corporate Finance   Case Study

while disclosing information to stakeholders. It had been providing consolidated financial statements under US GAAP to its global investors and financial statements under Indian GAAP to Indian shareholders. Infosys provided details on high and low monthly averages of share prices in all the stock exchanges on which the company's shares were listed. It was one of the few companies in India to provide segment wise breakup of revenues.

Code of Corporate Governance (Extract)

In the late 1990s, the Confederation of Indian Industries (CII) published a code of corporate governance (Refer Exhibit II for the highlights of the report). In 1999, the Securities and Exchange Board of India (SEBI) appointed a committee under the Chairmanship of Kumar Mangalam Birla5 to recommend a code of corporate governance. The report was submitted by the committee in November 1999 and accepted by SEBI in December 1999 (Refer Exhibit III for the highlights of the report).

Infosys had accepted the recommendation of both the CII and the Kumar Mangalam Birla Committee. The corporate governance practices followed by Infosys include the following:

1. Infosys had an executive chairman and chief executive officer (CEO) and a managing director, president and chief operating officer (COO). The CEO was responsible for corporate strategy, brand equity, planning, external contacts, acquisitions, and board matters. The COO was responsible for all day-to-day operational issues and achievement of the annual targets in client satisfaction, sales, profits, quality, productivity, employee empowerment and employee retention. The CEO, COO, executive directors and the senior management made periodic presentations to the board on their targets, responsibilities and performance.

2. The board members were expected to possess the expertise, skills and experience required to manage and guide a high growth, hi-tech software company. Expertise in strategy, technology, finance, and human resources was essential. They did not serve in any executive or non-executive position in any company in direct competition with Infosys.

3. Normally, the board meetings were scheduled at least a month in advance. Normally, the board met once a quarter to review the quarterly results and other issues. The board also met on the occasion of the annual shareholders' meeting. If the need arose, additional meetings were held. The non-executive directors had to attend at least four board meetings in a year. The board had access to any information that it wanted about the company.

4. In 2001, the board had three committees - the nominations committee, the compensation committee and the audit committee. To ensure independence of the

board, the members of the nominations committee, the compensation committee and the audit committee were all non-executive directors.

5. As per the recommendations of the Kumar Mangalam Committee, Infosys included a separate section on corporate governance in its annual report, which disclosed the remuneration paid to directors in all forms, including salary, benefits, bonuses, stock options. The annual report also carried a compliance certificate from the au

Some analysts felt that Infosys' corporate governance practices offered many lessons to corporate India. Infosys had shown that increasing shareholder wealth and safeguarding the interests of other stakeholders was not incompatible. Infosys had given its non-executive directors the mandate to pass judgement on the efficacy of its business plans. Every non-executive director not only played an active role in decision making, but also led or served on at least one of the three (Nomination, Compensation and Audit) committees. Infosys' founders had set very high standards, in a country where malpractices by founders were rampant. The founders only took salaries and dividends and derived no other financial benefits from the company.

Questions:
1. What is Corporate Governance?
2. Who are executive and non-executive board members?
3. What was the form of remuneration of the founders?
4. When was the first code of corporate governance published and by whom?

Case 3: Microsoft Corporation: Dividend Policy

In 2003, after it had completed 28 years, MSFT declared a cash dividend - the first time. It was the first of the listed company in DOW 30 which had not paid a cash dividend for such a long period. After 2003, the company's management started paying cash dividends as well as repurchasing common stock on a regular basis. On September 21, 2010, Microsoft Corporation (MSFT), the world's leading software company, increased its quarterly dividend by 23% to 16 cents from the 13 cents given the previous quarter. The management decided to raise a debt in order to pay the cash dividends. The company also announced a buyback of the common shares. On this occasion, Peter Klein (Klein), Chief Financial Officer of MSFT, said, "The increase of dividend was another sign, in addition to the company's share repurchase program, of Microsoft's commitment to shareholder value and confidence in its long-term growth prospects."

The management of the company decided to raise a debt of $6bn in order to pay for the dividends and the share buyback. During the financial year ending June 2010, the company paid a dividend of $0.52 per share to its ordinary shareholders.

Questions:

1. What was the dividend policy followed by Microsoft for 28 years?
2. What was the reason for the change in Dividend policy in the 2003?
3. Can a company increase the value of shareholders without paying them dividend?
4. Under what transactions did the company pay cash to the shareholders and how did it arrange cash resource?

***

Case study 4: Corporate Restructuring

Dabur India Ltd. initiated its demerger exercise in January 2003 after the agreement of the Board of Directors to hive of the Pharma business into a new company named Dabur Pharma Ltd. ("DPL"). After the demerger, Dabur FMCG concentrated on its core activities personal care, healthcare, and Ayurvedic specialities, while DPL focused on its expertise in oncology formulations and bulk drugs.

The demerger allowed investors to study the performance of these two entities with their respective industry standards.

The EVA and WACC of the demerged companies and composite figure of the company before demerger is given below:

	Dabur FMCG	DPL	Composite
EVA	51.18	−8.489	47.19
WACC	10.38%	11.31%	10.02%

Questions:

1. What is the technique of corporate restructure adopted by the company?
2. What are the possible reasons for the restructuring?
3. Was the company better off after restructuring? Give reasons.

***

www.ingramcontent.com/pod-product-compliance
Lightning Source LLC
Chambersburg PA
CBHW080351170426
43194CB00014B/2757